CUPCAKE O'CLOCK

CUPCAKE O'CLOCK

COLLINS & BROWN

The expression Good Housekeeping as used in the
title of the book is the trademark of The National
Magazine Company and The Hearst Corporation,
registered in the United Kingdom and USA, and
other principal countries of the world, and is the
absolute property of The National Magazine
Company and The Hearst Corporation. The use
of this trademark other than with the express
permission of The National Magazine Company
or The Hearst Corporation is strictly prohibited.

The Good Housekeeping website is
www.goodhousekeeping.co.uk

ISBN 978-1-909397-51-4

A catalogue record for this book is available from
the British Library.

Reproduction by Mission Productions Ltd,
Hong Kong
Printed and bound by 1010 Printing International Ltd

This book can be ordered direct from the publisher.
Contact the marketing department, but try your
bookshop first.

www.anovabooks.com

NOTES

Both metric and imperial measures are given for
the recipes. Follow either set of measures, not a
mixture of both, as they are not interchangeable.

All spoon measures are level.
1 tsp = 5ml spoon; 1 tbsp = 15ml spoon.

Ovens must be preheated to the specified
temperature.

Medium eggs should be used except where
otherwise specified. Free-range eggs are
recommended.

Use unwaxed lemons.

Note that some recipes contain raw or lightly
cooked eggs. The young, elderly, pregnant women
and anyone with an immune-deficiency disease
should avoid these because of the slight risk of
salmonella.

Contents

Classics

Icing and Frosting Cupcakes

The icing on cupcakes is now almost as important as the cake underneath. Icing helps keep the cake softer for longer (as long as the cakes are kept in their paper cases) and allows you to theme and decorate your cupcakes as desired.

Piping icing on to cupcakes

Many cupcake bakeries have developed a signature swirl of buttercream icing – practise and soon you'll have your own. Half-fill the piping bag with buttercream or frosting and hold the bag vertically as you pipe, squeezing gently from the top. Choose from the shapes below, or use your imagination.

Swirl

Fit a piping bag with a large star or plain nozzle. Starting from an outside edge, pipe an ever-decreasing circle on to the cupcake, slightly lifting the piping bag as you go. End with a point in the middle by sharply pulling away the piping bag.

Rosettes or blobs

The size of a rosette or blob depends on the nozzle used and the pressure applied to the piping bag. Fit the bag with a plain nozzle (to give blobs) or a star (to give rosettes). Holding the piping bag upright just above the surface, squeeze out some icing on to the cake (keeping the nozzle still). Pull up sharply to break the icing. Repeat the process to cover the cake surface with rosettes or blobs – it's easiest working in ever-decreasing circles. This method also looks good on the sides of a larger novelty or celebration cake.

Spreading

Start by gently brushing the top of the cooled cupcake with your finger or a brush to remove crumbs. Dollop a generous amount of buttercream or frosting on to the cake (it takes more than you might think) and gently spread the icing to the sides of the cake with a palette or butter knife for a smooth look. Alternatively, push the icing into a swirl or points with your spatula or knife.

Flooding cupcakes

Use a little less cake mixture when baking the cupcakes, so that when baked they don't quite reach the top of their cases. Spoon some glacé icing on top of the cooled cakes so that it floods out to the sides of the cases. Decorate with sprinkles, dragees, gold leaf or other decorations as desired.

Covering with sugarpaste

Covering cupcakes with sugarpaste works best if the baked cupcakes are flat – if they have peaked during baking, then trim to flatten. Next, simply roll out some sugarpaste in the desired colour, to a thickness of 5mm (¼in). Measure the top of the cupcakes, then cut out circles of sugarpaste to match. Spread a thin layer of buttercream over the cupcake, then secure the sugarpaste circle in place.

If you don't want to completely cover the tops with sugarpaste, cut out smaller shapes of the sugarpaste – hearts always look nice. Leave to dry completely on baking parchment. Position on buttercreamed cupcakes (the decorations should be stiff enough to stand up).

Perfect Piping

Making a paper icing bag

Reusable and disposable icing bags are available from all good cake decorating shops but it's just as easy to make your own from greaseproof paper. Once you have mastered the technique, make a batch so that you can swap between different coloured icings as you're working.

1 Cut out a rectangle of greaseproof paper 25.5 × 20.5cm (10 × 8in) – for smaller bags, cut a proportionally smaller rectangle. Fold in half diagonally, then tear or cut along the crease.

2 Put the paper on the worksurface with the apex of the triangle nearest to you. Bring the top left-hand point round to line up with the bottom point. Hold in place with your thumb and index finger.

3 Bring the right-hand point over and round the back, meeting at the bottom point. Pull together slightly to tighten the point.

4 Fold over the points of the paper nearest to you to secure the bag. To use, snip the point of the bag with scissors for different icing techniques (see page 8) or fit with metal nozzles for more intricate designs.

Filling a piping bag

Drop a nozzle into the end of the piping bag. If using a plastic piping bag, fold over the top to make a collar and, holding it in one hand, fill two-thirds with the icing. Fold over the top and gently press at the top to remove air bubbles and start the icing flowing.

Holding the piping bag

Hold the end of the bag in one hand. Squeeze from the top with your thumb. Rest the nozzle end in your other hand, using it to guide the bag. Squeeze gently for fine work, and apply slightly more pressure for thicker lines. To finish a line of piping cleanly, stop squeezing and pull away sharply.

Fairy Cakes

Hands-on time: 20 minutes
Cooking time: about 15 minutes, plus cooling and setting

125g (4oz) self-raising flour, sifted
1 tsp baking powder
125g (4oz) caster sugar
125g (4oz) unsalted butter, very soft
2 medium eggs
1 tbsp milk

For the icing and decoration
225g (8oz) icing sugar, sifted
assorted food colourings (optional)
sweets, sprinkles or coloured sugar

1 Preheat the oven to 200°C (180°C fan oven) mark 6. Line 18 of the holes in two bun tins with paper cases.

2 Using a hand-held electric whisk, beat the flour, baking powder, caster sugar, butter, eggs and milk in a large mixing bowl (or beat with a wooden spoon) for 2 minutes or until the mixture is pale and very soft. Half-fill each paper case with the mixture and bake for 10–15 minutes until golden brown. Transfer to a wire rack and leave to cool completely.

3 For the icing, put the icing sugar into a bowl and gradually blend in 2–3 tbsp warm water until the icing is fairly stiff, but spreadable. Add a couple of drops of food colouring, if you like.

4 Spread the top of each cake with the icing and decorate with sweets, sprinkles or coloured sugar.

Makes 18 fairy cakes or 12 cupcakes

Vanilla Cupcakes

Hands-on time: 15 minutes
Cooking time: 20 minutes, plus cooling and setting

125g (4oz) unsalted butter, softened

125g (4oz) golden caster sugar

2 medium eggs

125g (4oz) self-raising flour, sifted

1 tbsp vanilla extract

For the topping

200g (7oz) white chocolate, broken into pieces

1 Preheat the oven to 190°C (170°C fan oven) mark 5. Line a 12-hole bun tin or muffin tin with paper muffin cases.

2 Put the butter, sugar, eggs, flour and vanilla into a large bowl and beat thoroughly until smooth and creamy. Half-fill the paper cases with the mixture and bake for 15–20 minutes until pale golden, risen and springy to the touch. Transfer to a wire rack and leave to cool completely.

3 For the topping, melt the chocolate in a heatproof bowl set over a pan of gently simmering water, making sure the base of the bowl doesn't touch the water. Stir until smooth, then leave to cool slightly. Spoon the chocolate over the cakes and leave for about 1 hour to set.

Citrus Cupcakes

Hands-on time: 15 minutes
Cooking time: 20 minutes, plus cooling

125g (4oz) self-raising flour
1 tsp baking powder
125g (4oz) caster sugar
125g (4oz) soft margarine or
    unsalted butter
2 large eggs
grated zest of 2 large lemons, plus extra
    shreds, to decorate (optional)
1 tbsp freshly squeezed lemon juice

For the topping
1 × 125g (4oz) jar lemon curd
200ml (7fl oz) crème fraîche

1 Preheat the oven to 190°C (170°C fan oven) mark 5. Line a 12-hole muffin tin with paper muffin cases.

2 Sift the flour, baking powder and sugar into a large bowl, food processor or mixer. Add the margarine or butter, the eggs, lemon zest and juice and beat until light and fluffy. Divide the mixture equally among the paper cases and bake for about 20 minutes until firm to the touch and golden. Transfer to a wire rack and leave to cool completely.

3 For the topping, use a small, sharp knife to slice the top off each cake, then place a generous spoonful of lemon curd on top of the cake and put the lid back on. Add a dollop of crème fraîche, and a few tiny shreds of lemon zest, if you like.

Makes 12

Cherry Bakewell Cupcakes

Hands-on time: 30 minutes, plus chilling
Cooking time: 25 minutes, plus cooling and setting

175g (6oz) unsalted butter, softened

175g (6oz) caster sugar

3 medium eggs

150g (5oz) self-raising flour, sifted

1 tsp baking powder

75g (3oz) ground almonds

1 tsp almond extract

75g (3oz) glacé cherries, finely chopped

For the topping and decoration

1 tbsp custard powder

100ml (3½fl oz) milk

50g (2oz) unsalted butter, softened

250g (9oz) icing sugar, sifted

red sugar sprinkles

1 Preheat the oven to 190°C (170°C fan oven) mark 5. Line a 12-hole muffin tin with paper muffin cases.

2 Using a hand-held electric whisk, whisk the butter and caster sugar in a bowl (or beat with a wooden spoon) until pale and creamy. Gradually whisk in the eggs until just combined. Using a metal spoon, fold in the flour, baking powder, ground almonds, almond extract and cherries until combined. Divide the mixture equally among the paper cases and bake for 20 minutes or until golden and risen. Leave to cool in the tin for 5 minutes, then transfer to a wire rack and leave to cool completely.

3 For the topping, put the custard powder into a jug and add a little of the milk to make a smooth paste. Put the remaining milk into a pan and bring just to the boil. Pour the hot milk on to the custard paste and stir. Put back into the milk pan and heat gently for 1-2 minutes until it thickens. Take off the heat, cover with dampened

greaseproof paper to prevent a skin forming and leave to cool completely.

4 Put the custard into a bowl and, using a hand-held electric whisk, whisk in the butter (or beat with a wooden spoon). Chill for 30 minutes.

5 Gradually whisk the icing sugar into the chilled custard mixture until you have a smooth, thick icing. Using a small palette knife, spread a little custard cream over the top of each cake, then decorate with sugar sprinkles. Stand the cakes upright on the wire rack and leave for about 1 hour to set.

Makes 12

Coffee and Walnut Cupcakes

Hands-on time: 30 minutes, plus chilling
Cooking time: about 25 minutes, plus cooling

100g (3½oz) walnuts
175g (6oz) unsalted butter, softened
150g (5oz) self-raising flour, sifted
175g (6oz) light brown soft sugar
3 medium eggs
1 tsp baking powder
50ml (2fl oz) milk

For the topping and decoration
1 tbsp instant coffee granules
50g (2oz) unsalted butter, softened
200g (7oz) icing sugar, sifted
50g (2oz) walnuts, finely chopped

1 Preheat the oven to 190°C (170°C fan oven) mark 5. Line a 12-hole muffin tin with paper muffin cases.

2 Whiz the walnuts in a food processor until finely ground. Transfer to a large bowl. Add the butter, flour, brown sugar, eggs, baking powder and milk to the ground walnuts. Using a hand-held electric whisk, whisk together until pale and creamy (or beat with a wooden spoon). Divide the mixture equally among the paper cases and bake for 20–25 minutes until golden and risen. Leave to cool in the tin for 5 minutes, then transfer to a wire rack and leave to cool completely.

3 For the buttercream topping, put 2 tbsp boiling water into a small bowl, add the coffee and stir to dissolve. Put the butter, 100g (3½oz) of the icing sugar and the coffee mixture into a bowl and whisk until combined. Chill for 30 minutes.

4 Remove the buttercream from the fridge and gradually whisk in the remaining icing sugar until smooth and fluffy. Using a small palette knife, spread a little buttercream over the top of each cake. Put the chopped walnuts into a shallow bowl and lightly dip the top of each cake into the walnuts.

Makes 12

Raspberry Ripple Cupcakes

Hands-on time: 30 minutes
Cooking time: 20 minutes, plus cooling

50g (2oz) seedless raspberry jam

50g (2oz) fresh raspberries

125g (4oz) unsalted butter, softened

100g (3½oz) caster sugar

2 medium eggs

1 tbsp milk

150g (5oz) self-raising flour, sifted

For the topping and decoration

150g (5oz) fresh raspberries

300ml (½ pint) whipping cream

50g (2oz) icing sugar, sifted

1 Preheat the oven to 190°C (170°C fan oven) mark 5. Line a 12-hole muffin tin with 9 paper muffin cases.

2 Mix the raspberry jam with the raspberries, lightly crushing them. Put to one side.

3 Using a hand-held electric whisk, whisk the butter and caster sugar in a bowl (or beat with a wooden spoon) until pale and creamy. Gradually whisk in the eggs and milk until just combined. Using a metal spoon, fold in the flour until just combined, then carefully fold in the raspberry jam mixture until just marbled, being careful not to over-mix. Divide the mixture equally among the paper cases and bake for 20 minutes or until golden and risen. Leave to cool in the tin for 5 minutes, then transfer to a wire rack and leave to cool completely.

4 For the topping, keep 9 raspberries to one side. Mash the remaining raspberries in a bowl with a fork. Pass through a sieve into a bowl to remove the seeds. Using a hand-held electric whisk, whip the cream and icing sugar together until stiff peaks form. Mix the raspberry purée into the cream until combined.

5 Insert a star nozzle into a piping bag, then fill the bag with the cream and pipe a swirl on to the top of each cake. Decorate each with a raspberry.

Red Velvet Cupcakes

Hands-on time: 35 minutes
Cooking time: 25 minutes, plus cooling

150g (5oz) self-raising flour
1½ tbsp cocoa powder
a pinch of salt
150ml (¼ pint) buttermilk
¼ tsp red food colouring paste
100g (3½oz) unsalted butter, softened
150g (5oz) granulated sugar
2 medium eggs
1 tsp vanilla extract
¾ tsp white wine vinegar
¾ tsp bicarbonate of soda

For the icing

125g (4oz) unsalted butter, softened
300g carton full-fat cream cheese
75g (3oz) icing sugar
1 tsp vanilla extract
red sugar sprinkles (optional)

1 Preheat the oven to 180°C (160°C fan oven) mark 4 and line a 12-hole muffin tin with paper muffin cases. Sift the flour, cocoa and salt into a large bowl, then put to one side. Mix the buttermilk and food colouring paste in a small jug and put to one side.

2 In a separate large bowl, use a hand-held electric whisk to beat together the softened butter and granulated sugar until pale and fluffy – about 2 minutes. Add the eggs and vanilla and beat again. Alternately beat in one-third of the flour mixture and one-third of the buttermilk mixture. Continue until all the flour and buttermilk have been incorporated.

3 Quickly combine the vinegar and bicarbonate of soda in a small cup, then fold through the cake mixture. Divide the mixture equally among the paper cases and bake for 25 minutes or until a skewer inserted into the centre of the cakes comes out clean.

Transfer to a wire rack and leave to cool completely.

4 For the icing, beat the butter in a large bowl until smooth, then add the cream cheese and sift the icing sugar over. Mix until combined. Quickly beat in the vanilla. Pipe or smooth the icing over the cakes and scatter some sprinkles on top, if you like.

SAVE TIME

To get ahead, make the recipe to the end of step 3 up to one day in advance. Once cool, store the un-iced cakes in an airtight container. Ice the cakes up to 10 hours ahead, adding sprinkles at the last minute.

Makes 12

Modelling with Marzipan

Marzipan can be used to model decorations such as flowers, fruit and figurines. These modelled shapes are ideal for adding interest to cakes.

Working with marzipan

As marzipan generally only comes in white or yellow, it often needs to be coloured. To colour the marzipan, dip the tip of a cocktail stick into the desired shade of food colouring paste, then smear it on to the marzipan. Start with a little first, as you can always add more. Knead together until the desired shade is achieved.

(you might need to dust your hands with icing sugar to stop any sticking). When you have the desired shade, knead a small amount until soft and pliable, then roll or mould into shapes. Make sure you factor in at least 24 hours' drying time for marzipan shapes, so that the oil in the mixture will not soak into the iced cake.

To make marzipan carrots

1 Knead 65g (2½oz) marzipan until pliable. Add a dab of orange food colouring paste and knead evenly until distributed. Divide into 15 evenly sized pieces and roll each into a small cone. Put the cones on a tray lined with baking parchment.

2 Mark ridges down the top and sides of each cone to give the carrot life. Use a small amount of green marzipan or chopped angelica to make the top of the carrot. Leave to dry before using.

Ultimate Carrot Cupcakes

Hands-on time: 30 minutes
Cooking time: 20 minutes, plus cooling

150g (5oz) carrots
50g (2oz) raisins
175g (6oz) self-raising flour, sifted
½ tsp bicarbonate of soda
150g (5oz) light brown soft sugar
zest of 1 orange
½ tsp ground mixed spice
3 medium eggs
100ml (3½fl oz) sunflower oil
75ml (2½fl oz) buttermilk

For the topping and decoration

50g (2oz) icing sugar, sifted
250g (9oz) mascarpone cheese
100g (3½oz) quark cheese
juice of ½ orange
red, yellow and green ready-made
    fondant icing (optional)

1 Preheat the oven to 190°C (170°C fan oven) mark 5. Line a 12-hole muffin tin with paper muffin cases.

2 Coarsely grate the carrots and put into a large bowl. Add the raisins, flour, bicarbonate of soda, brown sugar, orange zest and mixed spice. Put the eggs, oil and buttermilk into a jug and lightly beat together until combined. Pour the egg mixture into the flour and stir with a spatula until just combined. Divide the mixture equally among the paper cases and bake for 20 minutes or until lightly golden and risen. Leave to cool in the tin for 5 minutes, then transfer to a wire rack and leave to cool completely.

3 For the topping, mix the sifted icing sugar with the mascarpone, quark and orange juice to a smooth icing. Using a small palette knife, spread a little of the icing over the top of each cake. Use the coloured fondant to make small carrots, if you like, and use to decorate the cakes.

Working with Chocolate

The type of chocolate you choose to work with will have a dramatic effect on the end product. For the best results, buy chocolate that has a high proportion of cocoa solids, preferably at least 70%. Most supermarkets stock a selection of different percentages. Chocolate with a high percentage of cocoa solids has a rich flavour and is perfect for cakes, sauces, ganache, most sweets and desserts. At the top end of the scale, couverture chocolate is the one preferred by chefs for confectionery work and gives an intense chocolate flavour that is probably best reserved for special mousses and gâteaux. It is available in milk, plain and white varieties from specialist chocolate shops. For most purposes, a good-quality chocolate with a high proportion of cocoa solids will usually give great results.

Melting chocolate

For making decorations or cooking, chocolate is usually melted first.

1. Break the chocolate into pieces and put into a heatproof bowl or in the top of a double boiler. Set over a pan of gently simmering water, making sure the base of the bowl doesn't touch the water.
2. Heat very gently until the chocolate starts to melt, then stir regularly until completely melted.

Variation

To melt chocolate in the microwave, break the chocolate into pieces and put in a microwave-proof bowl. Microwave at full power for 1 minute. Stir, then cook again for 30 seconds at a time until the chocolate is smooth and melted.

Notes

- ❑ When melting chocolate, use a gentle heat.
- ❑ Don't let water or steam touch the chocolate or it will become hard and unworkable. If it has 'seized', try stirring in a few drops of flavourless vegetable oil.

Chocolate Cupcakes

Hands-on time: 15 minutes
Cooking time: 20 minutes, plus cooling and setting

125g (4oz) unsalted butter, softened

125g (4oz) light muscovado sugar

2 medium eggs, beaten

15g (½oz) cocoa powder

100g (3½oz) self-raising flour

100g (3½oz) plain chocolate (at least 70% cocoa solids), roughly chopped

For the topping

150ml (¼ pint) double cream

100g (3½oz) plain chocolate (at least 70% cocoa solids), broken into pieces

1 Preheat the oven to 190°C (170°C fan oven) mark 5. Line a 12-hole and a 6-hole bun tin or muffin tin with paper muffin cases.

2 Beat the butter and sugar together until light and fluffy. Gradually beat in the eggs. Sift the cocoa powder with the flour and fold into the creamed mixture with the chopped chocolate. Divide the mixture equally among the paper cases and lightly flatten the surface with the back of a spoon. Bake for 20 minutes, then transfer to a wire rack and leave to cool completely.

3 For the topping, put the cream and chocolate into a heavy-based pan over a low heat and heat until melted, then leave to cool and thicken slightly. Spoon on to the cooled cakes, then stand the cakes upright on the wire rack and leave for 30 minutes to set.

Makes 18

Chocolate Butterfly Cakes

Hands-on time: 25 minutes
Cooking time: about 20 minutes, plus cooling

125g (4oz) unsalted butter, very soft

125g (4oz) caster sugar

2 medium eggs, lightly beaten
   individually

125g (4oz) plain flour

25g (1oz) cocoa powder

½ tsp baking powder

1 tbsp milk

For the buttercream

75g (3oz) unsalted butter, softened

175g (6oz) icing sugar, sifted

a few drops of vanilla extract

1–2 tbsp milk or water

1 Preheat the oven to 190°C (170°C fan oven) mark 5. Line 18 of the holes in two bun tins with paper cases.

2 Using a hand-held electric whisk, beat the butter and caster sugar together until soft and fluffy and lighter in colour. Beat in the eggs thoroughly, one at a time.

3 Sift the flour, cocoa powder and baking powder into the bowl and fold in gently until well mixed. Fold in the milk to give a soft, dropping consistency. Divide the mixture equally among the paper cases and bake for 15–20 minutes until risen and firm. Transfer to a wire rack and leave to cool completely.

4 To make the buttercream, put the butter into a bowl and beat with a wooden spoon or hand-held electric whisk until pale and creamy. Gradually stir in the icing sugar, followed by the vanilla and milk or water. Beat well until light and smooth. Either use immediately or cover well with clingfilm to exclude air.

5 Slice off the top of each cake and cut the slice in half. Using a palette knife, spread buttercream on each cake. Put the 'butterfly wings' on top, with their curved sides facing towards each other.

Makes 18

Black Forest Cupcakes

Hands-on time: 15 minutes
Cooking time: 20 minutes, plus cooling

85g (3oz) self-raising flour

4 tbsp cocoa powder

1 tsp baking powder

125g (4oz) caster sugar

125g (4oz) soft margarine or
unsalted butter

2 large eggs

For the topping and decoration

1 × 250g jar black cherry jam

200ml (7fl oz) double cream, whipped

50g (2oz) dark chocolate (at least
70% cocoa solids), grated

glacé cherries to decorate (optional)

1 Preheat the oven to 190°C (170°C fan oven) mark 5. Line a 12-hole muffin tin with paper muffin cases.

2 Sift the flour, cocoa powder, baking powder and sugar into a large bowl, food processor or mixer. Add the margarine or butter and the eggs and beat well until the mixture is pale and creamy. Divide the mixture equally among the paper cases and bake for about 20 minutes until firm to the touch. Transfer to a wire rack and leave to cool completely.

3 For the topping, cover the top of each cake with a generous amount of the jam – or you can use a jar of cherries that have been soaked in kirsch, if you like. Add the whipped cream and decorate with the grated chocolate, and a glacé cherry, if you like.

Makes 12

Time for a
Treat

Breakfast Cupcakes

🍴 **Hands-on time:** 30 minutes
Cooking time: 20 minutes, plus cooling and setting

175g (6oz) unsalted butter, softened

100g (3½oz) caster sugar

3 medium eggs

75g (3oz) apricot jam

150g (5oz) self-raising flour, sifted

75g (3oz) oatbran

½ tsp baking powder

For the icing and decoration

225g (8oz) icing sugar

1–2 tbsp orange juice

75g (3oz) mixed berry granola

1 Preheat the oven to 190°C (170°C fan oven) mark 5. Line a 12-hole muffin tin with paper muffin cases.

2 Using a hand-held electric whisk, whisk the butter and caster sugar in a bowl (or beat with a wooden spoon) until pale and creamy. Gradually whisk in the eggs until just combined. Using a metal spoon, fold in the apricot jam, flour, oatbran and baking powder until combined. Divide the mixture equally among the paper cases and bake for 20 minutes or until golden and risen. Leave to cool in the tin for 5 minutes, then transfer to a wire rack and leave to cool completely.

3 For the icing, sift the icing sugar into a bowl, then add enough orange juice to achieve a smooth, thick icing. Spoon a little on top of each cake, then sprinkle with the granola. Stand the cakes upright on the wire rack and leave for about 1 hour to set.

Makes 12

Toast and Marmalade Cupcakes

Hands-on time: 30 minutes
Cooking time: about 25 minutes, plus cooling and setting

150g (5oz) low-fat olive oil spread

200g (7oz) wholemeal self-raising flour, sifted

150g (5oz) light brown soft sugar

3 medium eggs

50g (2oz) marmalade

100ml (3½fl oz) milk

zest of 1 orange

50g (2oz) fresh wholemeal breadcrumbs

For the icing and decoration

125g (4oz) marmalade

300g (11oz) icing sugar, sifted

1 Preheat the oven to 180°C (160°C fan oven) mark 4. Line a 12-hole muffin tin with paper muffin cases.

2 Put the low-fat spread, flour, brown sugar, eggs, marmalade, milk, orange zest and breadcrumbs into a large bowl. Using a hand-held electric whisk, whisk together until pale and creamy (or beat with a wooden spoon). Divide the mixture equally among the paper cases and bake for 20–25 minutes until golden and risen. Leave to cool in the tin for 5 minutes, then transfer to a wire rack and leave to cool completely.

3 For the icing, pass the marmalade through a sieve into a bowl to remove the rind. Put the rind to one side. Mix the icing sugar with the sieved marmalade in a bowl until it forms a smooth icing. Spoon a little icing on to each cake to flood the top, then scatter the reserved rind over. Stand the cakes upright on the wire rack and leave for about 1 hour to set.

Go Nuts!

Nuts are used in many cupcakes. Some can be bought ready-prepared, but there are various tips and techniques that may be helpful.

Blanching and skinning

After nuts have been shelled, they are still coated with a skin, which, although edible, tastes bitter. This is easier to remove if the nuts are blanched or toasted.

1 **Blanching** Put the shelled nuts in a bowl and cover with boiling water. Leave for 2 minutes, then drain.
2 **Skinning** Remove the skins by rubbing the nuts in a teatowel or squeezing between your thumb and index finger.

Toasting

This also improves the flavour of nuts. Preheat the oven to 200°C (180°C fan oven) mark 6. Put the shelled nuts on a baking sheet in a single layer and bake for 8–15 minutes until the skins are lightly coloured. Remove the skins by rubbing the nuts in a teatowel.

1

2

Chopping

Unless you want very large pieces, the easiest way to chop nuts is in a food processor. Alternatively, place a chopping board on a folded teatowel on the worksurface and use a cook's knife. Only chop about 75g (3oz) nuts at a time.

1 Put the nuts in a food processor and pulse at 10-second intervals.
2 Chop to the size of coarse breadcrumbs. Store in an airtight container for up to two weeks.

Note: Leave nuts to cool completely after skinning and before chopping.

Storing nuts

Because of their high fat content, nuts do not keep particularly well and turn rancid if kept for too long.

Always buy nuts from a shop with a high turnover of stock so that you know they're likely to be fresh.

Store in an airtight container in a cool, dark place, or in the fridge, and use well within the 'best before' date on the pack.

Nutty Cupcakes

Hands-on time: 40 minutes
Cooking time: 25 minutes, plus cooling and setting

150g (5oz) unsalted butter, softened

175g (6oz) self-raising flour, sifted

50g (2oz) caster sugar

100ml (3½fl oz) golden syrup

3 medium eggs

1 tsp baking powder

1 tsp ground mixed spice

50g (2oz) mixed chopped nuts

For the topping

3 tbsp double cream

1 tbsp milk

50g (2oz) milk chocolate, finely chopped

25g (1oz) dark chocolate, finely chopped

75g (3oz) roasted chopped hazelnuts

1 Preheat the oven to 190°C (170°C fan oven) mark 5. Line a 12-hole muffin tin with paper muffin cases.

2 Put the butter, flour, sugar, syrup, eggs, baking powder, mixed spice and nuts into a large bowl. Using a hand-held electric whisk, whisk together until pale and creamy (or beat with a wooden spoon). Divide the mixture equally among the paper cases and bake for 20 minutes or until golden and risen. Leave to cool in the tin for 5 minutes, then transfer to a wire rack and leave to cool completely.

3 For the topping, heat the cream and milk in a small pan until nearly boiling. Put both chocolates into a heatproof bowl and pour the hot cream over them. Leave to stand for 5 minutes, then gently stir until smooth.

4 Put the hazelnuts into a shallow bowl. Dip the top of each cake into the chocolate cream, allow the excess to drip off, then dip into the hazelnuts until coated all over. Stand the cakes upright on the wire rack and leave for about 1 hour to set.

Easy Chocolate Cupcakes

Hands-on time: 20 minutes
Cooking time: 20 minutes, plus cooling

150g (5oz) unsalted butter, softened

150g (5oz) caster sugar

3 medium eggs, at room temperature

1 tsp vanilla extract

175g (6oz) self-raising flour

25g (1oz) cocoa powder

a pinch of salt

For the buttercream

150g (5oz) unsalted butter, at room temperature

300g (11oz) icing sugar, sifted

2 tbsp milk

1 Preheat the oven to 180°C (160°C fan oven) mark 4. Line a 12-hole bun tin with cupcake cases. Put the butter and caster sugar into a large bowl. Crack in the eggs and add the vanilla. Sift the flour, cocoa powder and salt over the mixture.

2 Using a hand-held electric whisk, whisk the ingredients together (or beat with a wooden spoon), then divide the mixture equally among the paper cases and bake for 15–20 minutes until firm and a skewer inserted into the centre of the cakes comes out clean. Transfer to a wire rack and leave to cool completely.

3 To make the buttercream, put the butter, icing sugar and milk into a large bowl and beat with an electric whisk. Spread some buttercream over the top of each cake and serve.

Makes 12

St Clements Cupcakes

Hands-on time: 40 minutes
Cooking time: about 18 minutes, plus cooling and setting

1 small orange (weight about 200g/7oz)
175g (6oz) self-raising flour, sifted
100g (3½oz) caster sugar
100ml (3½fl oz) milk
1 medium egg, beaten
50g (2oz) unsalted butter, melted
1 tsp baking powder
zest of 1 large lemon

For the topping and decoration

400g (14oz) royal icing sugar, sifted
zest and juice of 1 small orange
sugar star sprinkles
edible glitter (optional)

1 Preheat the oven to 190°C (170°C fan oven) mark 5. Line a 12-hole muffin tin with 9 paper muffin cases.
2 Grate the zest from the orange into a large bowl and put to one side. Cut the top and bottom off the orange and stand it upright on a board. Using a serrated knife, cut away the pith in a downward motion. Roughly chop the orange flesh, discarding any pips.

Put the chopped orange into a food processor and whiz until puréed. Transfer the orange purée into the bowl with the zest.
3 Add the flour, caster sugar, milk, egg, melted butter, baking powder and lemon zest. Stir with a spatula until just combined. Divide the mixture equally among the paper cases and bake for 15–18 minutes until golden and risen. Leave to cool in the tin for 5 minutes, then transfer to a wire rack and leave to cool completely.
4 For the topping, put the royal icing sugar, orange zest and juice into a bowl and whisk for 5 minutes or until soft peaks form. Spoon a little over the top of each cake to flood the top, then sprinkle with the stars. Stand the cakes upright on the wire rack and leave for about 1 hour to set. Dust with edible glitter, if you like, when set.

Makes 9

Orange and Poppy Seed Cupcakes

Hands-on time: 30 minutes
Cooking time: 20 minutes, plus cooling

175g (6oz) unsalted butter, softened

175g (6oz) caster sugar

3 medium eggs

175g (6oz) self-raising flour, sifted

grated zest and juice of 1 large orange

2 tbsp poppy seeds

1 tsp baking powder

For the icing and decoration

125g (4oz) unsalted butter, softened

250g (9oz) icing sugar, sifted

1 tbsp orange flower water

12 orange jelly slices and orange edible glitter (optional)

1 Preheat the oven to 190°C (170°C fan oven) mark 5. Line a 12-hole muffin tin with paper muffin cases.

2 Using a hand-held electric whisk, whisk the butter and caster sugar in a bowl (or beat with a wooden spoon) until pale and creamy. Gradually whisk in the eggs until just combined. Using a metal spoon, fold in the flour, orange zest and juice, poppy seeds and baking powder until combined. Divide the mixture equally among the paper cases and bake for 20 minutes or until golden and risen. Leave to cool in the tin for 5 minutes, then transfer to a wire rack and leave to cool completely.

3 For the icing, put the butter into a bowl and whisk until fluffy. Gradually add the icing sugar and orange flower water and whisk until light and fluffy.

4 Insert a star nozzle into a piping bag, then fill the bag with the buttercream and pipe a swirl on to the top of each cake. Decorate each with an orange slice and edible glitter, if you like.

Makes 12

Sour Cherry Cupcakes

Hands-on time: 30 minutes
Cooking time: about 20 minutes, plus cooling and setting

175g (6oz) unsalted butter, softened

175g (6oz) golden caster sugar

3 medium eggs

175g (6oz) self-raising flour, sifted

75g (3oz) dried cherries

2 tbsp milk

For the icing

225g (8oz) golden icing sugar, sifted

3 tbsp lemon juice, strained

1 Preheat the oven to 190°C (170°C fan oven) mark 5. Line a 12-hole bun tin or muffin tin with paper muffin cases.

2 Put the butter and caster sugar into a bowl and cream together until pale, light and fluffy. Beat in the eggs, one at a time, folding in 1 tbsp flour if the mixture looks as if it is about to curdle.

3 Put 12 dried cherries to one side. Fold the remaining flour and cherries and the milk into the creamed mixture until evenly combined. Divide the mixture equally among the paper cases and bake for 15–20 minutes until pale golden and risen. Transfer to a wire rack and leave to cool completely.

4 Put the icing sugar into a bowl and mix with the lemon juice to make a smooth dropping consistency. Spoon a little icing on to each cake and decorate each with a cherry, then stand the cakes upright on the wire rack and leave for about 1 hour to set.

Makes 12

Banoffee Cupcakes

Hands-on time: 30 minutes
Cooking time: 20 minutes, plus cooling

175g (6oz) self-raising flour, sifted
½ tsp bicarbonate of soda
150g (5oz) light brown soft sugar
1 banana (weight about 150g/5oz),
   peeled
3 medium eggs
100g (3½oz) unsalted butter, melted
75ml (2½fl oz) buttermilk

For the topping and decoration
150g (5oz) dulce de leche toffee sauce
75g (3oz) unsalted butter, softened
250g (9oz) golden icing sugar, sifted
mini fudge chunks (optional)

1 Preheat the oven to 190°C (170°C fan oven) mark 5. Line a 12-hole muffin tin with paper muffin cases.

2 Put the flour, bicarbonate of soda and brown sugar into a large bowl. Mash the banana with a fork in a small bowl. Put the eggs, melted butter and buttermilk into a jug and lightly beat together until combined. Pour into the flour mixture, add the mashed banana and stir with a spatula until just combined. Divide the mixture equally among the paper cases and bake for 18–20 minutes until lightly golden and risen. Leave to cool in the tin for 5 minutes, then transfer to a wire rack and leave to cool completely.

3 For the topping, whisk together the dulce de leche and butter in a bowl until combined. Gradually whisk in the icing sugar until light and fluffy. Using a palette knife, spread the buttercream on to the top of each cake, then decorate with the mini fudge chunks, if you like.

Makes 12

Apple Crumble Cupcakes

Hands-on time: 20 minutes
Cooking time: 25 minutes, plus cooling

320g (11½oz) eating apples, cored (about 2 apples)

juice of 1 lemon

200g (7oz) self-raising flour, sifted

1 tsp baking powder

1 tsp ground cinnamon

125g (4oz) light brown soft sugar

2 medium eggs

100g (3½oz) unsalted butter, melted

For the crumble

50g (2oz) plain flour

25g (1oz) unsalted butter, chilled and cut into cubes

15g (½oz) light brown soft sugar

1 Preheat the oven to 180°C (160°C fan oven) mark 4. Line a 12-hole muffin tin with paper muffin cases.

2 Make the crumble. Put the flour into a large bowl and, using your fingertips, rub in the butter until it resembles coarse breadcrumbs. Stir in the sugar and put to one side.

3 Coarsely grate the apples into a large bowl and mix in the lemon juice. Add the flour, baking powder, cinnamon and sugar. Put the eggs and melted butter into a jug and lightly beat together, then pour into the flour mixture. Stir with a spatula until just combined. Divide the mixture equally among the paper cases, then sprinkle the crumble equally over the top of each cake and bake for 25 minutes or until lightly golden and risen. Leave to cool in the tin for 5 minutes, then transfer to a wire rack and leave to cool completely.

Makes 12

Honeycomb Cream Cupcakes

Hands-on time: 30 minutes
Cooking time: 20 minutes, plus cooling

125g (4oz) unsalted butter, softened

50g (2oz) caster sugar

2 medium eggs

75g (3oz) runny honey

125g (4oz) self-raising flour, sifted

50g (2oz) rolled oats

½ tsp baking powder

1 tbsp milk

For the topping and decoration

125g (4oz) unsalted butter, softened

300g (11oz) golden icing sugar, sifted

2 tbsp milk

1 Crunchie bar, thinly sliced

1 Preheat the oven to 190°C (170°C fan oven) mark 5. Line a 12-hole muffin tin with 9 paper muffin cases.

2 Using a hand-held electric whisk, whisk the butter and caster sugar in a bowl (or beat with a wooden spoon) until pale and creamy. Gradually whisk in the eggs and honey until just combined. Using a metal spoon, fold in the flour, oats, baking powder and milk until combined. Divide the mixture equally among the paper cases and bake for 20 minutes or until golden and risen. Leave to cool in the tin for 5 minutes, then transfer to a wire rack and leave to cool completely.

3 For the topping, put the butter into a bowl and whisk until fluffy. Gradually whisk in half the icing sugar, then add the milk and the remaining icing sugar and whisk until light and fluffy.

4 Insert a star nozzle into a piping bag, fill with buttercream and pipe a swirl on to the top of each cake. Decorate each with a few slices of Crunchie.

Sticky Gingerbread Cupcakes

Hands-on time: 35 minutes
Cooking time: about 20 minutes, plus cooling

175g (6oz) self-raising flour

75g (3oz) unsalted butter, chilled and cut into cubes

¼ tsp bicarbonate of soda

2 tsp ground ginger

25g (1oz) preserved stem ginger in syrup, finely chopped, plus 3 tbsp syrup from the jar

50g (2oz) dark muscovado sugar

50g (2oz) golden syrup

50g (2oz) treacle

juice of 1 orange

2 medium eggs, beaten

For the topping and decoration

100g (3½oz) unsalted butter, softened

200g (7oz) icing sugar, sifted

3 tbsp syrup from the preserved stem ginger jar

1 tsp ground ginger

ready-made sugar flowers (optional)

1 Preheat the oven to 190°C (170°C fan oven) mark 5. Line a 12-hole muffin tin with 9 paper muffin cases.

2 Put the flour into a bowl and, using your fingertips, rub in the butter until it resembles breadcrumbs. Stir in the bicarbonate of soda, ground and stem ginger and set aside. Put the sugar, syrup, treacle and orange juice into a pan and heat gently until the sugar dissolves. Leave to cool for 5 minutes.

3 Mix the eggs and warm sugar mixture into the flour mixture and stir with a spatula until just combined. Divide the mixture equally among the paper cases and bake for 20 minutes or until golden and risen. Remove from the oven and drizzle each cake with 1 tsp ginger syrup. Leave to cool in the tin for 5 minutes, then transfer to a wire rack and leave to cool completely.

4 For the topping, put the butter into a bowl and whisk until fluffy. Add the icing sugar, ginger syrup and ground ginger and whisk until light and fluffy. Using a palette knife, spread a little topping over each cake. Decorate with sugar flowers, if you like.

Makes 9

Time for Tea

Modelling with Sugarpaste

Sugarpaste can be moulded or rolled thinly and dries without cracking, which makes it a good modelling material. Fully dried decorations will keep indefinitely if packed carefully in an airtight container – use bubble wrap or tissue paper to prevent breakages.

Sugarpaste can be bought in a variety of colours – or home-made sugarpaste can be easily dyed to the colour you want. If dyeing, add minute amounts of food colouring (pastes are ideal, see page 160) with the tip of a cocktail stick and knead in before adding any more. Before using sugarpaste for modelling, always knead it well first to help it soften and smooth.

When modelling with sugarpaste, always have some hard white vegetable fat to hand – a little smeared on the surface of your fingers will stop sugarpaste sticking without the paste drying out. As always when using sugarpaste, wrap any that you are not using in clingfilm to stop it drying out.

To make sugarpaste roses
You'll see many techniques for making moulded sugar roses, but it's about finding the method that suits you. The one detailed here is readily achievable and does not require specialist petal cutters.

1 Buy or colour sugarpaste to your desired shade. Make a cone of sugarpaste, which will form the centre of the rose, as well as the base for it to stand on while modelling. Take a pea-sized amount of your sugarpaste and shape into a petal in your palm, making it thicker at the base and finer at the rounded top edge. Wrap the first petal, thicker-part down, around the top part of your

cone to make the rose bud – the lower part of the cone holds the rose while modelling but will later be cut off.

2 Make another petal as before, then position it so that the centre of the second petal overlaps the join of the first one. Press one side on to the bud and leave the other slightly lifted off. Now make a third petal – slightly larger than the first two. Attach this petal by tucking it inside the lifted part of the second petal. Press gently around the bud at the base and bend the petals over a little at the top to give them movement.

3 Continue working around the rose as above. When the rose is the desired size, cut the rose at the base of the petals and place on a piece of foam pad to dry for at least 24–48 hours.

4 When dry, brush with lustres, if you like, and attach to your cake with a small dab of royal icing.

To make sugarpaste leaves

Buy or colour sugarpaste to your desired shade of green (alternatively, you can use white sugarpaste and later brush with a green food colouring dust). Lightly dust the worksurface with sifted icing sugar or cornflour, then roll out the sugarpaste thinly and stamp out shapes with a leaf cutter (plunge cutters are ideal for this, as they will imprint veins on to the leaf). If you don't have a leaf cutter, then use a small knife and imprint the veins manually.

Allow the leaves to dry flat on some baking parchment, or bend them over a piece of dowel or crumpled foil to give them movement.

3

Rosy Cupcakes

Hands-on time: about 25 minutes
Cooking time: about 20 minutes, plus cooling

175g (6oz) caster sugar

175g (6oz) unsalted butter, very soft but not melted

3 medium eggs, lightly beaten

175g (6oz) plain flour

1 tsp vanilla extract

1 tsp baking powder

For the icing

175g (6oz) caster sugar

4 medium egg whites

¼ tsp cream of tartar

250g (9oz) unsalted butter, at room temperature

1 tsp vanilla extract

pink food colouring paste

home-made or ready-made sugar roses (see page 68)

1 Preheat the oven to 180°C (160°C fan oven) mark 4. Line a 12-hole muffin tin with 12 paper muffin cases.

2 Using a hand-held electric whisk, beat the sugar and butter in a large bowl (or beat with a wooden spoon) until light and fluffy. Gradually beat in the eggs, a little at a time, folding in 1 tbsp flour if the mixture looks as if it's about to curdle. Beat in the vanilla extract.

3 Using a large metal spoon, fold in the flour, cocoa powder and baking powder. Divide the mixture evenly among the paper cases, filling them two-thirds full, and bake for 18–20 minutes until risen and a skewer inserted into the centre comes out clean. Transfer to a wire rack and leave to cool completely.

4 For the icing, put the sugar and 50ml (2fl oz) water into a pan and heat gently, stirring, to dissolve the sugar. When it has dissolved, increase the heat and bubble (without stirring) until the mixture reaches 115°C on a sugar thermometer.

5 Meanwhile, put the egg whites into a large heat-proof mixing bowl.

6 When the sugar mixture has reached the correct temperature, remove from the heat. Working quickly, use an

electric hand-held whisk to beat the egg whites until foamy, then add the cream of tartar and continue whisking until the egg whites hold stiff peaks.

7 With the mixer running at high speed, add the hot sugar syrup to the whites in a steady stream. Continue beating for 3 minutes or until the mixture is very thick and glossy and the base of the bowl doesn't feel warm.

8 While still mixing, gradually add the butter until it is all incorporated – don't worry if the mixture looks curdled, it will come back together with more beating. Continue mixing until the icing is thick, shiny and smooth – about 2 minutes. Beat in the vanilla and enough food colouring to the shade of pink you want.

9 Fill a piping bag fitted with an open star nozzle and pipe the icing on to the cupcakes. Decorate with sugar roses.

Makes 12

Perfect Decorations

If you don't have the time to decorate your cupcakes with hand-piped icing there are plenty of appealing alternatives.

Shortcut decorations

Fresh flowers make beautiful decorations for cupcakes. Ensure the flowers have not been sprayed with chemicals before decorating.

Ready-made sugar flowers are available from all good cake decorating shops and websites.

Fresh ribbons of coconut can look very pretty. Using a potato peeler, peel off thin ribbons of fresh coconut and arrange on top of the icing.

Ribbons are an effective finishing touch and can be colour themed to your cupcakes.

Crystallizing flowers and leaves

Edible flowers make a stunning individual decoration for cupcakes: rose petals and buds, daisies, pansies, violas and lavender sprigs are all suitable. Herbs, such as rosemary and mint, bay leaves and sweet geranium leaves; and fruit, such as grapes and redcurrants, can also be crystallized. They will keep for up to a week in a cool, dry place. Always use flowers and leaves that have not been sprayed with chemicals.

1 Lightly beat an egg white until slightly frothy. Using a small paintbrush, coat the flowers, leaves or fruit with the egg white.
2 Sprinkle with caster sugar to coat lightly and shake off the excess.
3 Leave to dry on baking parchment for two days in a cool, dry place (an airing cupboard or pantry is ideal) where they will crisp and harden.

Flower Cupcakes

Hands-on time: 15 minutes, plus drying
Cooking time: about 20 minutes, plus cooling and setting

175g (6oz) unsalted butter, softened
175g (6oz) golden caster sugar
3 medium eggs
175g (6oz) self-raising flour, sifted
finely grated zest and juice of 1 lemon

For the frosted flowers
1 medium egg white
6 edible flowers, such as violas
caster sugar to dust

For the icing
225g (8oz) icing sugar, sifted
1 drop of violet food colouring
2–3 tbsp lemon juice, strained

1 Preheat the oven to 190°C (170°C fan oven) mark 5. Line a 12-hole bun tin or muffin tin with paper muffin cases.

2 Put the butter and caster sugar into a bowl and cream together until pale, light and fluffy. Add the eggs, one at a time, and beat together, folding in 1 tbsp flour if the mixture looks as if it is about to curdle. Fold in the flour, lemon zest and juice and mix well. Divide the mixture equally among the paper cases and bake for 15–20 minutes until pale golden, risen and springy to the touch. Transfer to a wire rack and leave to cool completely.

3 To make the frosted flowers, whisk the egg white in a clean bowl for 30 seconds or until frothy. Brush over the flower petals and put on a wire rack resting on a piece of greaseproof paper. Dust heavily with caster sugar, then leave the flowers to dry.

4 To make the icing, put the icing sugar into a bowl with the food colouring. Mix in the lemon juice to make a smooth dropping consistency. Spoon the icing on to the cakes, then decorate with the frosted flowers. Stand the cakes upright on the wire rack and leave for about 1 hour to set.

Makes 12

Mini Green Tea Cupcakes

Hands-on time: 40 minutes
Cooking time: 25 minutes, plus cooling and infusing

100ml (3½fl oz) milk

2 tsp loose green tea leaves

100g (3½oz) unsalted butter, softened

125g (4oz) caster sugar

2 medium eggs

150g (5oz) self-raising flour, sifted

¼ tsp baking powder

For the topping and decoration

3 tsp loose green tea leaves

75g (3oz) unsalted butter, softened

250g (9oz) icing sugar, sifted

ready-made sugar flowers

1 Preheat the oven to 190°C (170°C fan oven) mark 5. Line a 12-hole muffin tin with paper fairy cake or bun cases.

2 Put the milk into a small pan and bring to the boil. Add the green tea leaves and leave to infuse for 30 minutes.

3 Using a hand-held electric whisk, whisk the butter and caster sugar in a bowl (or beat with a wooden spoon) until pale and creamy. Gradually whisk in the eggs until just combined. Pass the green tea milk through a sieve into the bowl, then discard the tea. Using a metal spoon, fold in the flour and baking powder until combined. Divide the mixture equally among the paper cases and bake for 18–20 minutes until golden and risen. Leave to cool in the tin for 5 minutes, then transfer to a wire rack and leave to cool completely.

4 For the topping, put the green tea leaves into a jug, add about 75ml (2½fl oz) boiling water and leave to infuse for 5 minutes. Put the butter into a bowl and whisk until fluffy. Gradually add the icing sugar and whisk until combined. Pass the green tea through a sieve into the bowl, then discard the tea. Continue to whisk until light and fluffy.

5 Insert a star nozzle into a piping bag, then fill the bag with the buttercream and pipe a swirl on to the top of each cake. Decorate each with a sugar flower.

Makes 12

Forest Fruit Cupcakes

Hands-on time: 25 minutes
Cooking time: about 20 minutes, plus cooling

175g (6oz) caster sugar

175g (6oz) unsalted butter, at room temperature

3 medium eggs, lightly beaten

175g (6oz) plain flour, sifted

finely grated zest of 1 lemon

1 tsp baking powder

100g (3½oz) seedless dark jam, such as blackcurrant

For the icing

200g (7oz) unsalted butter, at room temperature

1 tsp vanilla extract

375g (13oz) icing sugar, sifted

50g (2oz) fresh blackberries

1 Preheat the oven to 180°C (160°C fan oven) mark 4. Line a 12-hole muffin tin with paper muffin cases.

2 Using a hand-held electric whisk, beat the caster sugar and butter in a large bowl (or beat with a wooden spoon) for 3 minutes or until light and fluffy. Gradually add the eggs, whisking continuously and fold in 1 tbsp flour if the mixture looks as if it is about to curdle. Whisk in half the lemon zest.

3 Use a large metal spoon to fold in the flour and baking powder. Divide the mixture evenly among the paper cases and bake for 18–20 minutes until golden. Transfer to a wire rack and leave to cool completely.

4 Insert a 5–7mm (about ¼in) plain nozzle into a piping bag and spoon the jam into the bag. Push the piping nozzle into the middle of the top of each cake and squeeze a little jam into the centre.

5 For the icing, put the butter, vanilla, the remaining lemon zest and two-thirds of the icing sugar into a large bowl and

slowly beat with a hand-held electric whisk. Gradually beat in the remaining icing sugar until you have a soft but spreadable consistency that holds its shape. Briefly whisk in the fresh blackberries to get a marbled effect. Pipe or spread the icing on to the cakes and serve.

SAVE TIME

To get ahead, make the recipe to the end of step 3 up to one day in advance. Leave to cool completely, then transfer the cakes to an airtight container and store at room temperature. Complete the recipe to serve.

Makes 12

Lavender and Honey Cupcakes

Hands-on time: 35 minutes
Cooking time: about 20 minutes, plus cooling and setting

125g (4oz) unsalted butter, softened

125g (4oz) runny honey

2 medium eggs

125g (4oz) self-raising flour, sifted

1 tsp baking powder

For the icing and decoration

3 honey and lavender tea bags

2 tsp unsalted butter

250g (9oz) icing sugar, sifted

blue and red food colouring

purple sugar stars

edible silver dust (optional)

1 Preheat the oven to 190°C (170°C fan oven) mark 5. Line a 12-hole muffin tin with 9 paper muffin cases.

2 Using a hand-held electric whisk, whisk the butter and honey in a bowl (or beat with a wooden spoon) until combined. Gradually whisk in the eggs until just combined. Using a metal spoon, fold in the flour and baking powder until combined. Divide the mixture equally among the paper cases and bake for 15–20 minutes until golden and risen. Leave to cool in the tin for 5 minutes, then transfer to a wire rack and leave to cool completely.

3 For the icing, infuse the tea bags in 50ml (2fl oz) boiling water in a small bowl for 5 minutes. Remove the tea bags and squeeze out the excess water into the bowl. Stir in the butter until melted. Put the icing sugar into a large bowl, add the infused tea mixture and stir to make a smooth icing. Add a few drops of blue and red food colouring until it is lilac in colour.

4 Spoon a little icing on top of each cake, to flood the tops, then sprinkle with stars. Stand the cakes upright on the wire rack and leave for about 1 hour to set. Dust with edible dust, if you like, when set.

Makes 9

Ginger and Lemon Cupcakes

Hands-on time: 15 minutes
Cooking time: 20 minutes, plus cooling

125g (4oz) self-raising flour

125g (4oz) caster sugar

125g (4oz) soft margarine or
  unsalted butter

1 tsp baking powder

1 tsp ground ginger

grated zest of 1 lemon

2 large eggs

50g (2oz) crystallized (candied) ginger,
  chopped, plus extra to decorate

For the icing and decoration

200g (7oz) icing sugar, sifted

juice of 1 lemon

1 Preheat the oven to 190°C (170°C fan oven) mark 5. Line a 12-hole muffin tin with paper muffin cases.

2 Sift the flour and caster sugar into a large bowl, food processor or mixer. Add the margarine or butter, the baking powder, ground ginger, lemon zest and eggs and beat well until pale and creamy. Gently fold in the chopped crystallized ginger. Divide the mixture equally among the paper cases and bake for 20 minutes or until golden and firm to the touch. Transfer to a wire rack and leave to cool completely.

3 For the icing, put the icing sugar into a bowl, then slowly add the lemon juice and mix well. If you need a little more liquid, add a few drops of boiling water. Using a palette knife, spread the icing over each cake and top with a little chunk of the extra crystallized ginger.

Makes 12

Pistachio and Polenta Cupcakes

Hands-on time: 35 minutes
Cooking time: 25 minutes, plus cooling

150g (5oz) shelled pistachio nuts
175g (6oz) unsalted butter, softened
175g (6oz) caster sugar
3 medium eggs
200g (7oz) fine polenta
½ tsp baking powder
150g (5oz) ground almonds
zest of 2 lemons
2 tbsp milk

For the icing

75g (3oz) unsalted butter, softened
300g (11oz) icing sugar, sifted
juice of 2 lemons

1 Preheat the oven to 180°C (160°C fan oven) mark 4. Line a 12-hole muffin tin with paper muffin cases.
2 Whiz the pistachios in a food processor until really finely chopped.
3 Using a hand-held electric whisk, whisk the butter and caster sugar in a bowl (or beat with a wooden spoon) until pale and creamy. Gradually whisk in the eggs until just combined.

Using a metal spoon, fold in the polenta, baking powder, ground almonds, lemon zest, milk and 100g (3½oz) of the ground pistachios until combined. Divide the mixture equally among the paper cases and bake for 25 minutes or until golden and risen. Leave to cool in the tin for 5 minutes, then transfer to a wire rack and leave to cool completely.

4 For the icing, put the butter into a bowl and whisk until fluffy. Gradually whisk in half the icing sugar, then add the lemon juice and the remaining icing sugar, whisking until light and fluffy. Using a small palette knife, spread a little of the buttercream over the top of each cake, then sprinkle with a little of the remaining pistachios.

Makes 12

Coconut and Lime Cupcakes

Hands-on time: 30 minutes
Cooking time: about 20 minutes, plus cooling and setting

275g (10oz) plain flour, sifted

1 tbsp baking powder

100g (3½oz) caster sugar

zest of 1 lime

50g (2oz) desiccated coconut

2 medium eggs

100ml (3½fl oz) sunflower oil

225g (8oz) natural yogurt

50ml (2fl oz) milk

For the topping

150g (5oz) icing sugar, sifted

juice of 1 lime

50g (2oz) desiccated coconut

1 Preheat the oven to 200°C (180°C fan oven) mark 6. Line a 12-hole muffin tin with paper muffin cases.

2 Put the flour, baking powder, caster sugar, lime zest and coconut into a large bowl. Put the eggs, oil, yogurt and milk into a jug and lightly beat together until combined. Pour the yogurt mixture into the flour and stir with a spatula until just combined.

Divide the mixture equally among the paper cases and bake for 18–20 minutes until lightly golden and risen. Leave to cool in the tin for 5 minutes, then transfer to a wire rack and leave to cool completely.

3 For the topping, mix the icing sugar with the lime juice and 1–2 tsp boiling water to make a thick, smooth icing. Put the coconut into a shallow bowl. Dip each cake top into the icing until coated, allowing the excess to drip off, then carefully dip into the coconut until coated. Stand the cakes upright on the wire rack and leave for about 1 hour to set.

Chocolate Decorations

Chocolate decorations give an elegant, luxurious finish to
cakes. Avoid over-handling the finished decorations,
as chocolate melts and marks easily.

Chocolate wafers

1   You can make flat or curved wafers in any shape you like. Cut a piece of greaseproof paper to the required width.

2   Brush the paper evenly with melted chocolate and leave until the chocolate has almost set.

3   Using a knife, cut the chocolate (while still on the paper) into pieces of the desired size and shape (straight or curved, square or triangular, narrow or wide). You can also cut out chocolate shapes using small cutters.

4   Leave to cool and harden completely, either on the worksurface (for flat wafers) or draped over a rolling pin (for curled).

5   Carefully peel the wafers off the paper, handling them as little as possible, and store in the fridge for up to 24 hours.

Chocolate curls

1 Melt the chocolate (see page 33), then spread it out in a thin layer on a marble slab or clean worksurface. Leave to firm up.

2 Using a sharp, flat-ended blade (such as a pastry scraper or a very stiff spatula), scrape through the chocolate at a 45-degree angle. The size of the curls will be determined by the width of the blade.

Chocolate shavings

This is the easiest decoration of all because it doesn't call for melting the chocolate. Use chilled chocolate.

1 Hold a chocolate bar upright on the worksurface and shave pieces off the edge with a swivel peeler.

2 Alternatively, grate the chocolate, against a coarse or medium-coarse grater, to make very fine shavings.

Truffle Kisses Cupcakes

Hands-on time: 40 minutes
Cooking time: 30 minutes, plus cooling and setting

150g (5oz) unsalted butter, softened

200g (7oz) caster sugar

3 medium eggs

75g (3oz) self-raising flour, sifted

200g (7oz) plain flour, sifted

½ tsp bicarbonate of soda

75g (3oz) roasted chopped hazelnuts

200ml (7fl oz) buttermilk

15g (½oz) plain chocolate, finely grated

For the topping and decoration

200ml (7fl oz) double cream

150g (5oz) plain chocolate

100g (3½oz) milk chocolate, finely chopped

18 small chocolate truffles (optional)

1 Preheat the oven to 180°C (160°C fan oven) mark 4. Line a 12-hole and a 6-hole muffin tin with paper muffin cases.

2 Using a hand-held electric whisk, whisk the butter and sugar in a bowl (or beat with a wooden spoon) until pale and creamy. Gradually whisk in the eggs until just combined. Using a metal spoon, fold in both flours, the bicarbonate of soda, hazelnuts, buttermilk and grated chocolate until combined. Divide the mixture equally among the paper cases and bake for 20–25 minutes until golden and risen. Leave to cool in the tin for 5 minutes, then transfer to a wire rack and leave to cool completely.

3 For the topping, heat the cream in a small pan until nearly boiling. Finely chop 100g (3½oz) of the plain chocolate and put into a bowl along with all the milk chocolate. Pour the hot cream over the chocolate and leave to stand for 5 minutes, then stir gently

until smooth. Chill the mixture for 15–20 minutes until thickened slightly.

4 Using a palette knife, spread a little chocolate cream over the top of each cake. Finely grate the remaining plain chocolate over the top of each cake. Finish each with a chocolate truffle, if you like. Stand the cakes upright on the wire rack and leave for about 1 hour to set.

Makes 18

Party Time

Marbled Chocolate Cupcakes

Hands-on time: 40 minutes
Cooking time: 20 minutes, plus cooling

75g (3oz) unsalted butter, softened

150g (5oz) caster sugar

2 medium eggs

25g (1oz) self-raising flour, sifted

125g (4oz) plain flour, sifted

½ tsp bicarbonate of soda

2 tsp vanilla extract

150ml (¼ pint) buttermilk

25g (1oz) cocoa powder, sifted

For the topping

125g (4oz) unsalted butter, softened

350g (12oz) icing sugar, sifted

2 tsp vanilla extract

2 tbsp cocoa powder, sifted

1 Preheat the oven to 190°C (170°C fan oven) mark 5. Line a 12-hole muffin tin with paper muffin cases.

2 Using a hand-held electric whisk, whisk the butter and caster sugar in a bowl (or beat with a wooden spoon) until pale and creamy. Gradually whisk in the eggs until just combined. Using a metal spoon, fold in both flours, the bicarbonate of soda, vanilla and buttermilk until combined. Put half this mixture into another bowl and whisk in the cocoa powder. Then very lightly fold this mixture into the vanilla mixture, to create a marbled effect. Divide the mixture equally among the paper cases and bake for 20 minutes or until golden and risen. Leave to cool in the tin for 5 minutes, then transfer to a wire rack and leave to cool completely.

3 For the topping, put the butter into a bowl and whisk until fluffy. Gradually whisk in half the icing sugar, then add the vanilla, 2 tbsp boiling water and the remaining icing sugar and whisk until light and fluffy. Put half the mixture into another bowl and whisk in the cocoa powder.

4 Insert a star nozzle into a piping bag, then fill the bag alternately with the vanilla and chocolate buttercreams. Pipe a swirl on to the top of each cake.

Makes 12

Pavlova Cupcakes

Hands-on time: 30 minutes
Cooking time: 25 minutes, plus cooling and setting

125g (4oz) unsalted butter, softened

100g (3½oz) caster sugar

2 medium eggs

150g (5oz) self-raising flour, sifted

1 tbsp milk

zest of 1 lemon

50g (2oz) small fresh blueberries

12 fresh raspberries

For the frosting

1 medium egg white

175g (6oz) caster sugar

a pinch of cream of tartar

1 Preheat the oven to 190°C (170°C fan oven) mark 5. Line a 12-hole muffin tin with paper cases.

2 Using a hand-held electric whisk, whisk the butter and sugar in a bowl (or beat with a wooden spoon) until pale and creamy. Gradually whisk in the eggs until just combined. Using a metal spoon, fold in the flour, milk, lemon zest and blueberries until combined.

3 Divide the mixture equally among the paper cases and press 1 raspberry into the centre of each cake. Bake for 15 minutes or until golden and risen. Leave to cool in the tin for 5 minutes, then transfer to a wire rack and leave to cool completely.

4 For the frosting, put the egg white, sugar, 2 tbsp water and cream of tartar into a heatproof bowl and whisk lightly using a hand-held electric whisk. Put the bowl over a pan of simmering water and whisk continuously for about 7 minutes until the mixture thickens sufficiently to stand in peaks.

5 Insert a star nozzle into a piping bag, then fill the bag with the frosting and pipe a swirl on to the top of each cake. Stand the cakes upright on the wire rack and leave for about 1 hour to set.

Makes 12

Pretty Pink Cupcakes

Hands-on time: 35 minutes
Cooking time: 20 minutes, plus cooling

150g (5oz) raw beetroot, peeled and
  finely grated

200g (7oz) self-raising flour, sifted

½ tsp bicarbonate of soda

150g (5oz) caster sugar

zest of 1 orange

2 medium eggs

100ml (3½fl oz) sunflower oil

125ml (4fl oz) buttermilk

For the topping and decoration

100g (3½oz) unsalted butter, softened

350g (12oz) icing sugar, sifted

50ml (2fl oz) milk

pink food colouring

ready-made pink or red sugar flowers
  (optional)

1 Preheat the oven to 190°C (170°C fan
  oven) mark 5. Line a 12-hole muffin tin
  with paper muffin cases.

2 Put the beetroot, flour, bicarbonate of
  soda, caster sugar and orange zest into
  a bowl. Put the eggs, oil and buttermilk
  into a jug and lightly beat together
  until combined. Pour the egg mixture
  into the flour and stir with a spatula
  until just combined. Divide the mixture
  equally among the paper cases and
  bake for 20 minutes or until lightly
  golden and risen. Leave to cool in the
  tin for 5 minutes, then transfer to a wire
  rack and leave to cool completely.

3 For the topping, put the butter into a
  bowl and whisk until fluffy. Gradually
  whisk in half the icing sugar, then add
  the milk, a little pink food colouring
  and the remaining icing sugar and
  whisk until light and fluffy.

4 Insert a star nozzle into a piping bag,
  then fill the bag with the buttercream
  and pipe small swirls all the way
  around the top of each cake. Decorate
  with the sugar flowers, if you like.

Makes 12

American Frosting

To make 225g (8oz), enough to cover the top and sides of a 20.5cm (8in) cake, you will need: 1 large egg white, 225g (8oz) golden caster or granulated sugar, a pinch of cream of tartar.

1. Whisk the egg white in a clean, grease-free bowl until stiff. Put the sugar, 4 tbsp water and the cream of tartar into a heavy-based pan. Heat gently, stirring, until the sugar has dissolved. Bring to the boil, without stirring, and boil until the sugar syrup registers 115°C on a sugar thermometer.
2. Take off the heat and, as soon as the bubbles subside, pour the syrup on to the egg white in a thin stream, whisking constantly until thick and white. Leave to cool slightly.
3. When the frosting begins to turn dull around the edges and is almost cold, pour quickly over the cake and spread evenly with a palette knife.

Vanilla Icing

To make about 175g (6oz), enough to cover the top and sides of an 18cm (7in) cake, you will need: 150g (5oz) icing sugar, 5 tsp vegetable oil, 1 tbsp milk, a few drops of vanilla extract.

1. Sift the icing sugar into a bowl and, using a wooden spoon, beat in the oil, milk and vanilla extract until smooth.
2. Use the icing immediately, spreading it over the cake with a wet palette knife.

Coffee Fudge Icing

To make 400g (14oz), enough to cover the top and sides of a 20.5cm (8in) cake, you will need: 50g (2oz) unsalted butter, 125g (4oz) light muscovado sugar, 2 tbsp single cream or milk, 1 tbsp coffee granules, 200g (7oz) golden icing sugar, sifted.

1   Put the butter, muscovado sugar and cream or milk into a pan. Dissolve the coffee in 2 tbsp boiling water and add to the pan. Heat gently until the sugar dissolves, then bring to the boil and boil briskly for 3 minutes.
2   Take off the heat and gradually stir in the icing sugar. Beat well with a wooden spoon for 1 minute until smooth.
3   Use the frosting immediately, spreading it over the cake with a wet palette knife, or dilute with a little water to use as a smooth coating.

Variation
Omit the coffee. Add 75g (3oz) plain chocolate, in pieces, to the pan with the butter at the beginning of step 1.

Seven-minute Frosting

To make about 175g (6oz), enough to cover the top and sides of an 18cm (7in) cake, you will need: 1 medium egg white, 175g (6oz) caster sugar, a pinch of salt, a pinch of cream of tartar.

1. Put all the ingredients including 2 tbsp water into a heatproof bowl and whisk lightly using an electric or hand whisk.
2. Put the bowl over a pan of hot water, making sure the base of the bowl doesn't touch the water, and heat, whisking continuously, until the mixture thickens sufficiently to stand in peaks – this should take about 7 minutes.
3. Pour the frosting over the top of the cake and spread evenly with a palette knife.

Apricot Glaze

To make 450g (1lb), you will need:
450g (1lb) apricot jam, 2 tbsp water.

1. Put the jam and water into a pan and heat gently, stirring occasionally, until the jam has dissolved. Boil the jam rapidly for 1 minute, then strain through a sieve.

2. Using a wooden spoon, rub through as much fruit as possible. Discard the skins left in the sieve.

3. Pour the glaze into a clean, hot jar, then seal with a clean lid and leave to cool. Store in the fridge for up to two months. To use, brush over cakes before icing or applying almond paste, or use to glaze fruit finishes. If the consistency is a little stiff, then stir in a few drops of boiled water. You only need 3–4 tbsp apricot glaze for a 23cm (9in) cake, so this quantity will glaze 6–7 cakes.

Lemon and Vanilla Cupcakes

Hands-on time: 25 minutes
Cooking time: 15 minutes, plus cooling

200g (7oz) golden caster sugar

200g (7oz) unsalted butter, very soft

finely grated zest and juice of 1 lemon

4 medium eggs, beaten

200g (7oz) self-raising flour

For the icing and decoration

75g (3oz) unsalted butter, softened

175g (6oz) icing sugar, sifted

1–2 tbsp milk

1 tsp vanilla extract

selection of sugar sprinkles

1 Preheat the oven to 200°C (180°C fan oven) mark 6. Line a 12-hole muffin tin with paper muffin cases.

2 Using a hand-held electric whisk, whisk the caster sugar, butter and lemon zest in a large bowl (or beat with a wooden spoon) until pale and creamy. Beat in the eggs a little at a time, folding in 1 tbsp flour if the mixture looks as if it is about to curdle. Using a metal spoon, fold in the flour and lemon juice. Divide the mixture equally among the paper cases and bake for 12–15 minutes until golden. Transfer to a wire rack and leave to cool completely.

3 For the icing, put the butter into a large bowl and beat in two-thirds of the icing sugar, using a hand-held electric whisk. Gradually beat in the rest of the icing sugar with the milk and vanilla to make a soft but spreadable consistency that holds its shape.

4 When the cakes are completely cold, top each one with icing and swirl with a flat-bladed knife to form peaks. Decorate with sugar sprinkles.

Makes 12

Ginger and Orange Cupcakes

Hands-on time: 15 minutes
Cooking time: 20 minutes, plus cooling and setting

175g (6oz) unsalted butter, softened

175g (6oz) golden caster sugar

3 medium eggs

175g (6oz) self-raising flour, sifted

finely grated zest and juice of 1 orange

2 pieces of drained and chopped
preserved stem ginger, plus 1 piece
extra for decoration

For the icing and decoration

225g (8oz) icing sugar, sifted

2–3 tbsp orange juice, strained

1 Preheat the oven to 190°C (170°C fan oven) mark 5. Line a 12-hole muffin tin with paper muffin cases.

2 Using a hand-held electric whisk, whisk the butter and caster sugar in a bowl (or beat with a wooden spoon) until pale, light and fluffy. Add the eggs, one at a time, and beat together, folding in 1 tbsp flour if the mixture looks as if it is about to curdle. Fold in the flour, orange zest and juice and chopped stem ginger and mix well. Divide the mixture equally among the paper cases and bake for 15–20 minutes until pale golden, risen and springy to the touch. Transfer to a wire rack and leave to cool completely.

3 For the icing, put the icing sugar into a large bowl and mix in the orange juice to make a smooth dropping consistency. Spoon the icing on to the cakes, then decorate with finely chopped stem ginger. Stand the cakes on the wire rack and leave for about 1 hour to set.

Makes 12

Mango and Passion Fruit Cupcakes

Hands-on time: 30 minutes
Cooking time: 25 minutes, plus cooling

4 ripe passion fruit

about 75ml (2½fl oz) orange juice

150g (5oz) unsalted butter, softened

250g (9oz) plain flour, sifted

175g (6oz) caster sugar

3 medium eggs

1 tbsp baking powder

75g (3oz) ready to eat dried mango,
   finely chopped

For the topping and decoration

100g (3½oz) cream cheese

25g (1oz) unsalted butter, softened

200g (7oz) icing sugar, sifted

1 large ripe passion fruit

white sugar sprinkles

1 Preheat the oven to 180°C (160°C fan oven) mark 4. Line a 12-hole muffin tin with paper muffin cases.

2 Cut the passion fruit in half and pass the seeds and juice through a sieve into a jug. Discard the seeds. You need 150ml (¼ pint) liquid, so use the orange juice to top up the passion fruit juice.

3 Put the butter, flour, caster sugar, eggs, baking powder and passion fruit and orange juice into a large bowl. Using a hand-held electric whisk, whisk together (or beat with a wooden spoon) until pale and creamy. Add the mango and fold through until combined. Divide the mixture equally among the paper cases and bake for 25 minutes or until golden and risen. Leave to cool in the tin for 5 minutes, then transfer to a wire rack and leave to cool completely.

4 For the topping, whisk together the cream cheese and butter until fluffy. Gradually add the icing sugar until combined. Cut the passion fruit in half and pass the seeds and juice through a sieve into the icing. Discard the seeds. Stir to combine, then, using a small palette knife, spread a little over the top of each cake. Scatter the sugar sprinkles over each cake.

Makes 12

Tropical Burst Cupcakes

Hands-on time: 35 minutes
Cooking time: 20 minutes, plus cooling and setting

200g (7oz) self-raising flour, sifted

½ tsp bicarbonate of soda

100g (3½oz) caster sugar

50g (2oz) ready-to-eat dried tropical fruit, finely chopped

3 medium eggs

100ml (3½fl oz) sunflower oil

75ml (2½fl oz) buttermilk

227g can pineapple pieces, drained and finely chopped

For the topping and decoration

225g (8oz) royal icing sugar, sifted

zest and juice of 1 lime

sugar decorations (optional)

1 Preheat the oven to 190°C (170°C fan oven) mark 5. Line a 12-hole muffin tin with paper muffin cases.

2 Put the flour, bicarbonate of soda, caster sugar and dried fruit into a large bowl. Put the eggs, oil and buttermilk into a jug and lightly beat together until combined. Pour the oil mixture and the pineapple pieces into the flour and stir with a spatula until just combined. Divide the mixture equally among the paper cases and bake for 20 minutes or until lightly golden and risen. Leave to cool in the tin for 5 minutes, then transfer to a wire rack and leave to cool completely.

3 For the topping, put the icing sugar, lime juice and zest and 1 tbsp cold water into a bowl and whisk for 5 minutes or until soft peaks form. Using a small palette knife, spread a little over the top of each cake. Stand the cakes upright on the wire rack, scatter with sugar decorations, if you like, and leave for about 1 hour to set.

Makes 12

Aniseed Cupcakes

Hands-on time: 30 minutes
Cooking time: about 25 minutes, plus cooling

125g (4oz) unsalted butter, softened

200g (7oz) caster sugar

2 medium eggs

200g (7oz) self-raising flour, sifted

25g (1oz) custard powder

2 tbsp caraway seeds

125ml (4fl oz) milk

For the topping and decoration

75g (3oz) unsalted butter, softened

300g (11oz) icing sugar, sifted

2 tbsp Pernod

pale blue sugar sprinkles

1 Preheat the oven to 190°C (170°C fan oven) mark 5. Line a 12-hole muffin tin with paper muffin cases.

2 Using a hand-held electric whisk, whisk the butter and caster sugar in a bowl (or beat with a wooden spoon) until pale and creamy. Gradually whisk in the eggs until just combined. Using a metal spoon, fold in the flour, custard powder, caraway seeds and milk until combined. Divide the mixture equally among the paper cases and bake for 20–25 minutes until golden and risen. Leave to cool in the tin for 5 minutes, then transfer to a wire rack and leave to cool completely.

3 For the topping, put the butter into a bowl and whisk until fluffy. Gradually whisk in half the icing sugar, then add the Pernod, 1 tbsp boiling water and the remaining icing sugar and whisk until light and fluffy. Using a small palette knife, spread a little of the buttercream over the top of each cake, then sprinkle with the blue sugar sprinkles.

Makes 12

Sea Breeze Cupcakes

Hands-on time: 40 minutes
Cooking time: 20 minutes, plus cooling and setting

1 pink grapefruit (weight about 350g/12oz)
50g (2oz) ready to eat dried cranberries
250g (9oz) self-raising flour, sifted
125g (4oz) caster sugar
50ml (2fl oz) milk
1 medium egg, beaten
75g (3oz) unsalted butter, melted
1 tsp baking powder

For the icing and decoration

300g (11oz) fondant icing sugar, sifted
red and yellow food colouring
50g (2oz) apricot glaze (see page 105)
edible silver balls
cocktail umbrellas (optional)

1 Preheat the oven to 190°C (170°C fan oven) mark 5. Line a 12-hole muffin tin with paper muffin cases.

2 Grate the zest from half the grapefruit into a bowl. Put to one side. Cut the top and bottom off the grapefruit and stand it upright on a board. Using a serrated knife, cut away the pith in a downward motion. Cut in between the membranes to remove the segments. Whiz the segments in a food processor until puréed.

3 Transfer the purée into the bowl with the zest. Add the cranberries, flour, caster sugar, milk, egg, melted butter and baking powder and stir with a spatula until just combined. Divide the mixture equally among the paper cases and bake for 20 minutes or until golden and risen. Leave to cool in the tin for 5 minutes, then transfer to a wire rack and leave to cool completely.

4 For the icing, put the icing sugar into a bowl and add enough water (2–4 tbsp) to make a smooth icing. Add a few drops of food colouring to make it pinky-orange in colour. Brush the tops of the cakes with the apricot glaze, then spoon a little icing on to each cake to flood the top. Decorate with the silver balls. Stand the cakes upright on the wire rack and leave for about 1 hour to set. Decorate with a cocktail umbrella once set, if you like.

Jewelled Cupcakes

Hands-on time: 40 minutes
Cooking time: 30 minutes, plus cooling and setting

75g (3oz) unsalted butter, softened

150g (5oz) caster sugar

3 medium eggs

175g (6oz) self-raising flour, sifted

175g (6oz) mincemeat

For the decoration

75g (3oz) apricot glaze (see page 105)

50g (2oz) toasted flaked almonds

50g (2oz) ready to eat apricots, chopped

12 glacé cherries

40g (1½oz) caster sugar

1 tbsp unsalted butter

1 Preheat the oven to 190°C (170°C fan oven) mark 5. Line a 12-hole muffin tin with paper muffin cases.

2 Using a hand-held electric whisk, whisk the butter and sugar in a bowl (or beat with a wooden spoon) until pale and creamy. Gradually whisk in the eggs until just combined. Using a metal spoon, fold in the flour and mincemeat until combined. Divide the mixture equally among the paper cases and bake for 20 minutes or until golden and risen. Leave to cool in the tin for 5 minutes, then transfer to a wire rack and leave to cool completely.

3 For the decoration, brush each cake with a little apricot glaze, then scatter on a few almonds and apricots and a cherry. Stand the cakes upright on the wire rack.

4 Put the sugar and 1 tbsp cold water into a small pan and gently heat until the sugar dissolves. Increase the heat and bubble for 3–4 minutes until the sugar caramelizes and turns golden in colour. Take off the heat and quickly stir in the butter until combined. Being very careful, drizzle the hot caramel over the top of each cake. Leave for about 10 minutes to set.

Makes 12

Star Cupcakes

Hands-on time: 40 minutes
Cooking time: 20 minutes, plus cooling and drying

125g (4oz) unsalted butter, softened

125g (4oz) caster sugar

2 large eggs

grated zest and juice of 1 large lemon

125g (4oz) self-raising flour

1 tsp baking powder

For the icing and decoration

225g (8oz) fondant sugar

cornflour to dust

125g (4oz) sugarpaste

edible glue

edible glitter in silver and gold

1 Preheat the oven to 180°C (160°C fan oven) mark 4. Line a 12-hole muffin tin with paper muffin cases.

2 Using a hand-held electric whisk, whisk the butter and caster sugar in a large bowl (or beat with a wooden spoon) until light and fluffy. Beat the eggs in a separate bowl, then gradually add them to the butter and sugar mixture, beating well between each addition. Add the lemon zest and beat well.

3 Sift in the flour and baking powder and fold in with a large metal spoon. If the mixture needs loosening a bit, add a little lemon juice. The mixture should gently drop off a spoon. Divide the mixture equally among the paper cases and bake for 20 minutes or until firm to the touch and golden. Transfer to a wire rack and leave to cool completely.

4 Make up the fondant icing following the instructions on the pack. Ice the cupcakes when cold and leave to dry.

5 Dust a worksurface with cornflour and roll out the sugarpaste until it is about 3mm ($\frac{1}{8}$in) thick. Using a star-shaped cutter, cut out 12 star shapes.

6 Using a small paintbrush, paint edible glue over each star, making sure they are completely covered, then dip 6 stars in gold glitter and 6 in silver glitter. Dab a tiny bit of edible glue on the centre of each cupcake and carefully place a star on top.

Makes 12

Wedding Cupcakes

Hands-on time: 30 minutes
Cooking time: about 15 minutes, plus cooling and setting

1 × quantity cupcake mixture
(see Fairy Cakes, page 14)

For the icing and decoration
pink food colouring paste
500g (1lb 2oz) buttercream
(see page 36)
12 rose-themed cupcake surrounds
home-made or ready-made sugar hearts
(see page 68)

FREEZE AHEAD

It is best to decorate these cupcakes on the day that they're needed, but the undecorated cakes can be made and frozen ahead. Bake, cool and freeze the cupcakes up to one month before the event. When needed, allow the cakes to thaw at room temperature before decorating.

1 Make the cupcakes as described on page 14, using 12 pink paper cupcake cases. Leave to cool completely before decorating.

2 For the icing, dip the tip of a cocktail stick into the desired shade of pink food colouring, then dip into the buttercream. Use a spatula to start mixing in the colour, stopping when the buttercream is marbled.

3 Insert a 1cm (½in) open-star nozzle into a piping bag and fill the bag with the buttercream. Hold the piping bag just above the centre of a cupcake and start piping with even pressure. Swirl the icing in a spiral from the centre towards the edges, making sure the entire surface of the cake is covered. By starting in the centre (rather than the outside edge as is normal) you should create a rose effect. Repeat with the remaining cupcakes. Leave to set for at least 1 hour.

4 Fit the surrounds around the cupcakes. Decorate with sugar hearts.

Makes 12

Kids o'clock

Sweet Shop Cupcakes

🍴 **Hands-on time:** 30 minutes
Cooking time: 20 minutes, plus cooling and setting

175g (6oz) unsalted butter, softened

175g (6oz) caster sugar

3 medium eggs

175g (6oz) self-raising flour, sifted

zest of 1 lemon

½ tsp baking powder

125g (4oz) lemon curd

For the topping and decoration

75g (3oz) unsalted butter, softened

350g (12oz) icing sugar, sifted

50ml (2fl oz) milk

dolly mixtures, jelly beans or
 chocolate buttons

1 Preheat the oven to 190°C (170°C fan
  oven) mark 5. Line a 12-hole muffin tin
  with paper muffin cases.

2 Using a hand-held electric whisk,
  whisk the butter and caster sugar in
  a bowl (or beat with a wooden spoon)
  until pale and creamy. Gradually
  whisk in the eggs until just combined.
  Using a metal spoon, fold in the flour,
  lemon zest and baking powder until
  combined. Divide the mixture equally
  among the paper cases and bake for
  20 minutes or until golden and risen.
  Leave to cool in the tin for 5 minutes,
  then transfer to a wire rack and leave
  to cool completely.

3 Cut a small cone shape from the top of
  each cake. Put a teaspoonful of lemon
  curd into the hole in each cake and
  then replace the cake cone, pressing
  down lightly.

4 For the topping, put the butter into a
  bowl and whisk until fluffy. Gradually
  add half the icing sugar, whisking
  until combined. Add the milk and
  remaining icing sugar and whisk
  until light and fluffy, then, using a
  small palette knife, spread a little over
  each cake. Stand the cakes upright
  on the wire rack and leave for about
  30 minutes to set. Decorate each cake
  with sweets when set.

Makes 12

Rocky Road Cupcakes

Hands-on time: 30 minutes
Cooking time: about 20 minutes, plus cooling and setting

100g (3½oz) unsalted butter, softened

125g (4oz) caster sugar

2 medium eggs

150g (5oz) self-raising flour, sifted

25g (1oz) glacé cherries, diced

25g (1oz) milk chocolate chips

25g (1oz) pinenuts

For the topping

100g (3½oz) milk chocolate

50ml (2fl oz) double cream

25g (1oz) mini marshmallows

25g (1oz) glacé cherries, finely chopped

1 × 37g bag Maltesers

1 Preheat the oven to 190°C (170°C fan oven) mark 5. Line a 12-hole muffin tin with 9 paper muffin cases.

2 Using a hand-held electric whisk, whisk the butter and sugar in a bowl (or beat with a wooden spoon) until pale and creamy. Gradually whisk in the eggs until just combined. Using a metal spoon, fold in the flour, cherries, chocolate chips and pinenuts until combined. Divide the mixture equally among the paper cases. and bake for 15–20 minutes until golden and risen. Leave to cool in the tin for 5 minutes, then transfer to a wire rack and leave to cool completely.

3 For the topping, break the chocolate into pieces, then put into a heatproof bowl with the cream. Set over a pan of gently simmering water, making sure the base of the bowl doesn't touch the water. Heat until melted, stirring occasionally until smooth.

4 Take off the heat and, using a small palette knife, spread a little over the top of each cake. Decorate each with marshmallows, cherries and Maltesers. Stand the cakes upright on the wire rack and leave for about 1 hour to set.

Makes 9

Polka Dot Cupcakes

Hands-on time: 30 minutes
Cooking time: 20 minutes, plus cooling

250g (9oz) plain flour, sifted

1 tbsp baking powder

100g (3½oz) caster sugar

1 tbsp vanilla extract

2 medium eggs

125ml (4fl oz) sunflower oil

175g (6oz) natural yogurt

For the topping and decoration

50g (2oz) unsalted butter, softened

175g (6oz) icing sugar, sifted

25g (1oz) cocoa powder, sifted

mini Smarties or chocolate beans

1 Preheat the oven to 190°C (170°C fan oven) mark 5. Line a 12-hole muffin tin with paper muffin cases.

2 Put the flour, baking powder and caster sugar into a large bowl. Put the vanilla, eggs, oil and yogurt into a jug and lightly beat together until combined. Pour into the flour mixture and stir with a spatula until just combined. Divide the mixture equally among the paper cases and bake for 20 minutes or until lightly golden and risen. Leave to cool in the tin for 5 minutes, then transfer to a wire rack and leave to cool completely.

3 For the topping, put the butter into a bowl and whisk until fluffy. Gradually add the icing sugar until combined. Add the cocoa powder and 2 tbsp boiling water and whisk until light and fluffy. Using a small palette knife, spread a little buttercream over the top of each cake. Decorate with mini Smarties or chocolate beans.

Makes 12

Mallow Madness Cupcakes

Hands-on time: 40 minutes
Cooking time: about 25 minutes, plus cooling and setting

3 medium eggs
175g (6oz) self-raising flour, sifted
150g (5oz) caster sugar
175ml (6fl oz) sunflower oil
½ tsp baking powder
50g (2oz) white chocolate chips

For the topping and decoration
125g (4oz) pink and white marshmallows
1 medium egg white
150g (5oz) caster sugar
a pinch of cream of tartar
pink sugar sprinkles

1 Preheat the oven to 190°C (170°C fan oven) mark 5. Line a 12-hole muffin tin with paper muffin cases.
2 Using a hand-held electric whisk, whisk the eggs, flour, sugar, oil and baking powder in a large bowl (or beat with a wooden spoon) until just combined. Add the chocolate chips and fold through. Divide the mixture equally among the paper cases and bake for 20–25 minutes until lightly golden and risen. Leave to cool in the tin for 5 minutes, then transfer to a wire rack and leave to cool completely.
3 For the topping, keep 6 white marshmallows to one side. Put the remaining marshmallows, the egg white, sugar and cream of tartar into a heatproof bowl and whisk lightly using a hand-held electric whisk. Put the bowl over a pan of simmering water and whisk continuously, for about 7 minutes until the marshmallows have melted and the mixture thickens sufficiently to stand in peaks.
4 Cut the reserved marshmallows in half. Using a small palette knife, spread a little of the icing over the top of each cake. Scatter with sugar sprinkles and top each with a marshmallow half. Stand the cakes upright on the wire rack and leave for about 1 hour to set.

Makes 12

Peanut Butter Cupcakes

Hands-on time: 30 minutes
Cooking time: 25 minutes, plus cooling and setting

75g (3oz) unsalted peanuts or cashew nuts, toasted

100g (3½oz) unsalted butter, softened

50g (2oz) light brown soft sugar

50g (2oz) dark muscovado sugar

3 medium eggs

175g (6oz) self-raising flour, sifted

½ tsp baking powder

For the topping and decoration

100ml (3½fl oz) milk

50g (2oz) cocoa powder

300g (11oz) icing sugar

100g (3½oz) peanut butter

chocolate sprinkles or vermicelli

1 Preheat the oven to 190°C (170°C fan oven) mark 5. Line a 12-hole muffin tin with paper muffin cases.

2 Whiz the peanuts or cashews in a food processor until finely ground. Put to one side.

3 Using a hand-held electric whisk, whisk the butter with the light brown and muscovado sugars (or beat with a wooden spoon) until pale and creamy. Gradually whisk in the eggs until just combined. Using a metal spoon, fold in the flour, baking powder and finely ground nuts until combined. Divide the mixture equally among the paper cases and bake for 20 minutes or until golden and risen. Leave to cool in the tin for 5 minutes, then transfer to a wire rack and leave to cool completely.

4 For the topping, warm the milk in a small pan. Sift the cocoa powder and icing sugar into a large bowl, then gradually stir in the warm milk until it forms a smooth icing.

5 Put a small spoonful of peanut butter on the top of each cake and then spoon the chocolate icing on to cover the peanut butter and to coat the top of the cake. Decorate with sprinkles or vermicelli. Stand the cakes upright on the wire rack and leave for about 1 hour to set.

Makes 12

Cookies and Cream Cupcakes

Hands-on time: 30 minutes
Cooking time: about 20 minutes, plus cooling

75g (3oz) mini Oreo cookies

175g (6oz) unsalted butter, softened

150g (5oz) caster sugar

3 medium eggs

175g (6oz) self-raising flour, sifted

½ tsp baking powder

3 tbsp milk

½ tsp vanilla extract

For the topping

75g (3oz) unsalted butter, softened

150g (5oz) icing sugar, sifted

2 tsp vanilla extract

1 tsp cocoa powder

1 Preheat the oven to 200°C (180°C fan oven) mark 6. Line a 12-hole muffin tin with paper muffin cases. Keep 12 mini cookies to one side and roughly chop the remainder.

2 Using a hand-held electric whisk, whisk the butter and caster sugar in a bowl (or beat with a wooden spoon) until pale and creamy. Gradually whisk in the eggs until just combined. Using a metal spoon, fold in the flour, baking powder, milk, vanilla and chopped cookies until combined. Divide the mixture equally among the paper cases and bake for 15–20 minutes until golden and risen. Leave to cool in the tin for 5 minutes, then transfer to a wire rack and leave to cool completely.

3 For the topping, put the butter into a bowl and whisk until fluffy. Gradually add the icing sugar and vanilla and whisk until light and fluffy. Using a small palette knife, spread the buttercream over the top of each cake. Sift a little cocoa powder on to the top of each cake and then decorate each with a reserved Oreo cookie.

Makes 12

Chocolate Fairy Cakes

Hands-on time: 20 minutes
Cooking time: about 15 minutes, plus cooling and setting

100g (3½oz) self-raising flour

25g (1oz) cocoa powder

1 tsp baking powder

125g (4oz) caster sugar

125g (4oz) unsalted butter, very soft

2 medium eggs

1 tbsp milk

50g (2oz) chocolate drops

For the icing and decoration

225g (8oz) icing sugar, sifted

assorted food colourings (optional)

sweets, sprinkles or coloured sugar

1 Preheat the oven to 200°C (180°C fan oven) mark 6. Line 18 of the holes in two bun tins with paper cases.

2 Sift the flour into a mixing bowl, then sift in the cocoa powder, baking powder and caster sugar. Add the butter, eggs and milk and beat with a hand-held electric whisk (or use a wooden spoon) for 2 minutes or until the mixture is pale and very soft. Stir in the chocolate drops and divide equally among the paper cases, then bake for 10–15 minutes until risen and springy to the touch. Transfer to a wire rack and leave to cool completely.

3 For the icing, put the icing sugar into a bowl and gradually blend in 2–3 tbsp warm water until the icing is fairly stiff, but spreadable. Add a couple of drops of food colouring, if you like.

4 Using a small palette knife, spread the icing on the tops of the cakes, then decorate with sweets, sprinkles or coloured sugar.

Makes 18

Red Nose Buns

Hands-on time: 20 minutes
Cooking time: about 15 minutes, plus cooling and setting

50g (2oz) unsalted butter, very soft

50g (2oz) caster sugar

1 medium egg, beaten

50g (2oz) self-raising flour

¼ tsp baking powder

1 ripe banana, peeled and mashed

For the icing and decoration

125g (4oz) icing sugar, sifted

about 1 tbsp orange juice

red glacé cherries or round red
  jelly sweets

1 Preheat the oven to 190°C (170°C fan oven) mark 5. Arrange about 36 petits fours cases on baking sheets.

2 Put the butter, caster sugar, egg, flour and baking powder into a food processor and whiz until smooth and well mixed. Add the banana and whiz for 1 minute. Put a teaspoonful of the mixture into each paper case and bake for 12–15 minutes until golden. Transfer to a wire rack and leave to cool completely.

3 For the icing, mix the icing sugar with the orange juice until smooth and just thick enough to coat the back of a spoon. Top each bun with a small blob of icing and stick half a glacé cherry or a jelly sweet on each one. Stand the cakes upright on the wire rack and leave for about 1 hour to set.

Makes 36

Secret Garden Cupcakes

Hands-on time: 45 minutes
Cooking time: 50 minutes, plus cooling

200g (7oz) fresh strawberries,
  hulled and halved

200g (7oz) caster sugar

150g (5oz) unsalted butter, softened

3 medium eggs

200g (7oz) self-raising flour, sifted

½ tsp bicarbonate of soda

50ml (2fl oz) buttermilk

For the topping and decoration

125g (4oz) unsalted butter, softened

250g (9oz) icing sugar, sifted

green food colouring

sugar ladybird, bumble bee and butterfly
  decorations (optional)

1 Preheat the oven to 190°C (170°C fan
  oven) mark 5. Line a 12-hole muffin tin
  with paper muffin cases.

2 Put the strawberries and 50g (2oz) of
  the caster sugar into a heatproof bowl
  and cover with clingfilm. Put over a
  pan of barely simmering water and
  cook gently for 30 minutes.

3 Meanwhile, using a hand-held electric
  whisk, whisk the butter and remaining
  caster sugar in a bowl (or beat with a
  wooden spoon) until pale and creamy.
  Gradually whisk in the eggs until just
  combined. Using a metal spoon, fold
  in the flour, bicarbonate of soda and
  buttermilk until combined. Divide
  the mixture equally among the paper
  cases and bake for 20 minutes or until
  golden and risen. Leave to cool in the
  tin for 5 minutes. Meanwhile, pass
  the strawberries and juice through a
  sieve into a shallow bowl. Discard the
  strawberries.

4 Using a cocktail stick, prick the top of
  the cakes all over. Dip the top of each
  cake into the strawberry syrup, then
  transfer to a wire rack and leave to
  cool completely.

5 For the buttercream topping, put the
  butter into a bowl and whisk until
  fluffy. Gradually whisk in half the
  icing sugar, then add 1 tbsp boiling

water, a little green food colouring and the remaining icing sugar and whisk until light and fluffy.

6 Insert a star nozzle into a piping bag, then fill the bag with the buttercream and pipe in a zigzag pattern on top of each cake. Decorate with the sugar ladybirds, butterflies and bumble bees, if you like.

Makes 12

Fairy-tale Flower Cupcakes

Hands-on time: 15 minutes
Cooking time: 20 minutes, plus cooling and setting

125g (4oz) self-raising flour, sifted

125g (4oz) caster sugar, sifted

1 tsp baking powder

125g (4oz) soft margarine or
    unsalted butter

2 large eggs

1 tsp vanilla extract

For the icing and decoration

200g (7oz) icing sugar, sifted

gel food colouring

12 sugar roses

1 Preheat the oven to 180°C (160°C fan oven) mark 4. Line a 12-hole muffin tin with paper muffin cases.

2 Put the flour, caster sugar, baking powder, margarine or butter, the eggs and vanilla into a mixer and beat until the mixture is pale and creamy. Divide heaped teaspoons of the mixture among the paper cases and bake for 20 minutes or until golden, and firm and springy to the touch. Transfer the cakes to a wire rack and leave to cool completely.

3 For the icing, put the icing sugar in a bowl and slowly add enough boiling water until it is a thick soup consistency. Add the food colouring and pour over the cakes. Leave for about 10 minutes, then carefully place a rose on top of each cake.

Makes 12

Kitten Cupcakes

Hands-on time: 25 minutes
Cooking time: 20 minutes, plus cooling

125g (4oz) unsalted butter, very soft

125g (4oz) caster sugar

grated zest of 1 lemon

2 medium eggs, beaten

125g (4oz) self-raising flour, sifted

For the icing and decoration

175g (6oz) icing sugar

black and assorted writing icings

jelly diamonds and Smarties

black liquorice laces, cut into
short lengths

1 Preheat the oven to 190°C (170°C fan oven) mark 5. Line a 12-hole bun tin with paper cases.

2 Using a hand-held electric whisk, whisk the butter, caster sugar and lemon zest in a bowl (or beat with a wooden spoon) until light and fluffy. Add the eggs, a little at a time, beating well after each addition. Using a metal spoon, fold in the flour. Divide the mixture equally among the paper cases and bake for 20 minutes or until golden and risen. Transfer to a wire rack and leave to cool completely.

3 For the icing, sift the icing sugar into a bowl. Stir in 1–2 tbsp warm water, a few drops at a time, until you have a smooth, spreadable icing. If necessary, slice the tops off the cooled cakes to make them level. Using a small palette knife, spread the top of each cake with icing.

4 Decorate the cakes to make kittens' faces. Use black writing icing for the eyes, halve the jelly diamonds for the ears, press a Smartie in the centre for a nose, and use black writing icing to draw on a mouth. Use different coloured writing icing for the pupils and markings. Press on liquorice whiskers.

Makes 12

Seasonal Sweets

Be Mine Cupcakes

Hands-on time: 30 minutes
Cooking time: 15 minutes, plus cooling

125g (4oz) unsalted butter, softened

100g (3½oz) caster sugar

2 medium eggs

125g (4oz) self-raising flour, sifted

½ tsp baking powder

1 × 51g bar Turkish Delight, finely chopped

1 tbsp rosewater

For the topping and decoration

75g (3oz) unsalted butter, softened

250g (9oz) icing sugar, sifted

2 tbsp rosewater

pink and white heart-shaped sugar sprinkles

about 12 Loveheart sweets (optional)

1 Preheat the oven to 190°C (170°C fan oven) mark 5. Line a 12-hole muffin tin with paper cases.

2 Using a hand-held electric whisk, whisk the butter and caster sugar in a bowl (or beat with a wooden spoon) until pale and creamy. Gradually whisk in the eggs until just combined. Using a metal spoon, fold in the flour, baking powder, Turkish Delight and rosewater until combined. Divide the mixture equally among the paper cases and bake for 15 minutes or until golden and risen. Leave to cool in the tin for 5 minutes, then transfer to a wire rack and leave to cool completely.

3 For the topping, put the butter into a bowl and whisk until fluffy. Add the icing sugar and rosewater and whisk until light and fluffy. Using a small palette knife, spread a little buttercream over the top of each cake. Decorate with sugar hearts, then top each with a Loveheart, if you like.

Valentine Cupcakes

🍴 **Hands-on time:** 30 minutes
Cooking time: 20 minutes, plus cooling

oil to grease

125g (4oz) self-raising flour

125g (4oz) caster sugar

1 tsp baking powder

125g (4oz) soft margarine or
    unsalted butter

2 large eggs

1 tsp vanilla extract

For the glacé icing

225g (8oz) icing sugar, sifted

juice of 1 large lemon or 2 tbsp
    boiling water

gel food colouring of your choice

For the decoration

food colouring of your choice
    (preferably gel)

edible glue

red edible glitter

1 Preheat the oven to 190°C (170° fan oven) mark 5. Carefully oil a 12-hole straight-sided silicone heart-shaped muffin tray. Have ready 10 metallic foil cupcake cases.

2 Sift the flour, caster sugar and baking powder into a bowl, food processor or mixer. Add the margarine or butter, the eggs and vanilla and beat until pale and creamy. Spoon the mixture carefully into the muffin tray, place on a metal baking sheet and bake for 20 minutes or until golden and firm to the touch. Leave to cool in the muffin tray, then turn the cupcakes out on to a wire rack and leave to cool completely.

3 To create a level surface, slice the tops off the cupcakes and turn the cakes upside down (you will be icing the bottom of the cakes).

4 To make the glacé icing, put the icing sugar in a bowl and slowly add the lemon juice or boiling water, a little at a time. Stir until smooth (stop adding

the liquid once the icing is a smooth, spreadable consistency) and tint it to your chosen colour. Drizzle the icing all over the cakes and let it run down the sides.

5 Before the icing is completely dry, lay out the metallic cupcake cases. Dip your fingers into a bowl of cold water, then lift the cakes on to the cases (this stops the icing sticking to your fingers). Carefully mould the cases around the hearts.

6 When the icing is completely dry, paint the entire top with edible glue and dip into the glitter.

Makes 10

Mother's Day Cupcakes

Hands-on time: 20 minutes
Cooking time: about 12 minutes, plus cooling and setting

100g (3½oz) unsalted butter, softened

100g (3½oz) caster sugar

100g (3½oz) self-raising flour

2 medium eggs

For the icing and decoration

125g (4oz) icing sugar, sifted

pink and green food colouring

hundreds and thousands

1 Preheat the oven to 200°C (180°C fan oven) mark 6. Line 20 holes of a mini muffin tin or cupcake tin with mini paper muffin or cupcake cases. If you don't have one, put the cases (two cases thick) directly on a baking sheet.

2 Put the butter, caster sugar, flour and eggs into a large bowl and beat with a wooden spoon until mixed. Divide the mixture equally among the paper cases and bake for 10–12 minutes until golden and a skewer inserted into the centre of the cakes comes out clean. Transfer the cakes (still in their cases) to a wire rack and leave to cool completely.

3 For the icing, divide the icing sugar between two bowls. If using liquid food colouring, add a little pink to one bowl and green to the other, then stir to check the consistency. To each bowl, add just enough water to bring the mixture together to a smooth, spoonable consistency. If using colouring pastes, dye white icings, already at the right consistency, by dipping the end of a cocktail stick into dyes, then into the icing. Stir to mix.

4 Cover the top of each cake with green or pink icing, then sprinkle with hundreds and thousands. Serve or leave to set first.

Makes 20

Easter Cupcakes

Hands-on time: 30 minutes
Cooking time: 30 minutes, plus cooling and setting

2 medium eggs
75g (3oz) caster sugar
150ml (¼ pint) sunflower oil
150g (5oz) plain flour, sifted
½ tsp baking powder
1 tsp vanilla extract
15g (½oz) Rice Krispies

For the topping and decoration

100g (3½oz) white chocolate, broken
  into pieces
15g (½oz) unsalted butter
25g (1oz) Rice Krispies
12 chocolate mini eggs

1 Preheat the oven to 180°C (160°C fan oven) mark 4. Line a 6-hole muffin tin with paper muffin cases.

2 Separate the eggs, putting the whites in a clean, grease-free bowl and the egg yolks in another. Add the sugar to the yolks and whisk with a hand-held electric whisk until pale and creamy. Then whisk in the oil until combined.

3 Whisk the egg whites until soft peaks form. Using a metal spoon, quickly fold the flour, baking powder, vanilla and Rice Krispies into the egg yolk mixture until just combined. Add half the egg whites to the egg yolk mixture to loosen, then carefully fold in the remaining egg whites. Divide the mixture equally among the paper cases and bake for 20–25 minutes until golden and risen. Leave to cool in the tin for 5 minutes, then transfer to a wire rack and leave to cool completely.

4 For the topping, put the chocolate and butter into a heatproof bowl and

place over a pan of barely simmering water, making sure the base of the bowl doesn't touch the water. Gently heat until the chocolate has melted, stirring occasionally until smooth. Take the bowl off the heat, add the Rice Krispies and fold through until coated. Spoon the mixture on top of each cake, pressing down lightly, then top each with 2 chocolate eggs. Stand the cakes upright on the wire rack and leave for about 1 hour to set.

Makes 6

Halloween Cupcakes

🍴 **Hands-on time:** 1 hour
Cooking time: about 20 minutes, plus cooling

175g (6oz) caster sugar

175g (6oz) unsalted butter, very soft but not melted

3 medium eggs, lightly beaten

150g (5oz) plain flour

1 tsp vanilla extract

25g (1oz) cocoa powder

1 tsp baking powder

For the icing

200g (7oz) unsalted butter, very soft

350g (12oz) icing sugar

a few drops of orange food colouring

For the decoration

100g (3½oz) plain chocolate (or use orange and black sprinkles)

1 Preheat the oven to 180°C (160°C fan oven) mark 4. Line a 12-hole muffin tin with 12 muffin or cupcake cases.

2 Using a hand-held electric whisk, beat the sugar and butter in a large bowl (or beat with a wooden spoon) until light and fluffy. Gradually beat in the eggs, a little at a time, folding in 1 tbsp flour if the mixture looks as if it's about to curdle. Beat in the vanilla extract.

3 Using a large metal spoon, fold in the flour, cocoa and baking powder. Divide the mixture evenly among the paper cases, filling them two-thirds full, and bake for 18–20 minutes until risen and a skewer inserted into the centre comes out clean. Transfer to a wire rack and leave to cool completely.

4 For the icing, beat together the butter and icing sugar until pale. Add a few drops of food colouring and 1 tsp hot water, then beat until smooth and creamy. Insert a large star nozzle into a piping bag, then fill the bag with icing and pipe swirls of icing on to the cooled cupcakes.

5 To make chocolate Halloween decorations, draw some simple shapes such as bats, ghosts, moons and cats. Trace four of each design on to a sheet of baking parchment (a few will serve as spares), then place the parchment

on a baking sheet or tray. Melt the chocolate in a heatproof bowl set over a pan of hot water, or in short spurts in the microwave. Spoon the melted chocolate into a paper piping bag and snip off the merest fraction of the tip. Pipe over the outline of each shape and over the eyes of the ghosts. Snip a fraction more off the tip and fill in the shapes with more chocolate. Leave in a cool place (or in the fridge) until set. Carefully peel away the lining paper.

6 Gently press a chocolate decoration on top of each cupcake, or simply top with orange and black sprinkles.

Makes 12

Take 5 Colour It

There has been quite a revolution in the food colouring industry over the past few years. Nearly gone are the watery liquids in a limited range of colours that dilute the mediums we were trying to colour, rather than tint them. These have been replaced with a range of vibrant pastes, powders and concentrated liquid colours and pens. Visit a specialist cake shop or website, as there are so many great products to help you create stunning cake designs.

Liquid colours

Liquid colours tend to be cheaper and more suitable for adding to cake mixes than to icing. Add drop by drop to achieve the desired colour – but care must be taken, as they can easily dilute the mixtures (and can cause mixtures to curdle if too much is added). They are available from most supermarkets in a wide range of everyday colours.

Paste colours

These very concentrated moist pastes come in every possible colour you can need. They are ideal for colouring buttercream, sugarpaste and royal icing, as well as flower paste and marzipan. They are so concentrated that they will not affect the consistency of the mixture regardless of the depth of colour required. Apply with a cocktail stick a dot at a time until you have reached the desired shade. The pastes can also be applied neat with a paintbrush to add fine definition to work. When colouring with dark food colouring pastes, the colour can deepen on standing. Ideally (if using dark shades), tint to a shade lighter than the ultimate desired shade, then cover the icing/marzipan and leave to stand for 2–3 hours before using.

Colour dusts

These edible powdered food colourings are suitable for kneading into sugarpaste, brushing to add colour to finished decorations, or for shading and colouring base icings on cakes. Dip a brush into the dust, then work the brush into or over the icing. A vast range of colours is available.

Try stencilling food colouring dusts on to the surface of a sugarpasted cake. Dampen a sponge or piece of muslin and wring out well. Scrunch it up and dab quickly into the food dust. Lightly dab the surface of the sugarpaste to imprint the colour. Re-dip into the colour as necessary. Always practise on an unwanted scrap of sugarpaste first to achieve the desired technique.

Food colouring pens

These pens are filled with a variety of liquid food colourings. Their consistency can be a little unreliable when writing on sugarpaste, royal icing or marzipan, but they can be useful for adding small colour accents to sugarcraft.

Lustre colours

These edible food colourings come in different powdered finishes – pearl, iridescent, metallic and sparkle. They give subtle colour with a high-sheen finish and are non-water soluble. The real advantage of these lustre colours is that they can be brushed on to dried decorations that have been made out of white sugar- or flower paste. Different colours and shades may be applied to give a realistic effect.

Perfect Royal Icing

This is a traditional white icing made from sugar, lemon juice and egg whites, which dries to a hard finish. Royal icing is used for covering cakes and also for piping decorations.

Royal Icing

Royal icing can also be bought in packs from supermarkets. Simply add water or egg white to use.

To make 450g (1lb) you will need: 2 medium egg whites, ¼ tsp lemon juice, 450g (1lb) icing sugar, sifted, 1 tsp glycerine.

1 Put the egg whites and lemon juice into a clean bowl and stir to break up the egg whites. Add sufficient icing sugar to mix to the consistency of pouring cream. Continue mixing and adding small quantities of icing sugar until the desired consistency is reached, mixing well and gently beating after each addition. The icing should be smooth, glossy and light, almost like a cold meringue in texture, but not aerated. Do not add the icing sugar too quickly or it will produce a dull heavy icing. Stir in the glycerine until well blended. (Alternatively, for large quantities of royal icing, use a food mixer on the lowest speed, following the same instructions as before.)

2 Leave the icing to settle before using it; cover the surface with a piece of damp clingfilm and seal well, excluding all the air.

3 Stir the icing thoroughly before use to disperse any air bubbles, then, if necessary, adjust the consistency by adding more sifted icing sugar.

Piping nozzles
Star nozzle
The star nozzle is the most versatile of all the metal nozzles. By varying the pressure and angle, you can produce many designs, including scallops, fluted lines, rosettes and shells.

Fluted line
Holding the piping bag at a 45-degree angle and 5mm (¼in) above the surface, pipe towards yourself, raising the bag slightly as the icing flows on to the surface. Pull away sharply to finish.

Piping with royal icing
1   Don't overfill the piping bag, otherwise icing will spill over the top. Messy hands will disturb your concentration and blobs of icing could fall on your design.
2   Keep the work area as clean as possible to avoid mess or blemishes on the cake.
3   Cover the bowl of icing with a damp teatowel or kitchen paper to stop it drying out while you are piping.
4   Plan your pattern before piping. Prick out the design with a pin to give you a template to follow.

Rosette

Holding the piping bag vertically and just above the surface, squeeze the bag gently until you have the sized rosette you need, then lift away.

Cable

Holding the piping bag at a 45-degree angle and 5mm (¼in) above the surface, pipe to the left then right in a slight zigzag motion.

Spiral

Holding the piping bag at a 45-degree angle and 5mm (¼in) above the surface, pipe a short line towards yourself, then lift the nozzle up and over the previous line in an arc. Continue piping in arcs, gradually increasing in size as you reach the middle and decreasing in size towards the end.

Shells

Holding the piping bag at a 45-degree angle and 5mm (¼in) above the surface, pipe a small blob of icing, then bring the bag up and towards you and back down to the surface. Pull away sharply. Pipe the next shell over the end of the previous one.

Lattice
Pipe straight vertical and horizontal lines in a crisscross pattern.

Other nozzles
Once you have mastered the basic techniques of icing, you might want to experiment with other nozzles that can produce ribbon, frills, ruffles and leaves.

Piping – what went wrong?
Before using any piping equipment, it is essential to have the icing at the correct consistency. When a wooden spoon is drawn out of royal icing, it should form a fine but sharp point. If the icing is too stiff it will be very difficult to pipe; if too soft, the icing will be difficult to control and the piped shapes will lose their definition.

Always remember, the larger the nozzle the stiffer the icing, and for a very fine nozzle the consistency needs to be slightly softer.

The lines have broken
❑ The icing was too stiff
❑ The icing was pulled along rather than allowed to flow from the piping bag
❑ There were too many bubbles in the icing

The lines are wobbly
❑ The bag was squeezed too hard
❑ The icing was too runny

The lines are flat
❑ The icing was too runny
❑ The nozzle was held too near the surface of the icing

Bonfire Night Cupcakes

Hands-on time: 30 minutes
Cooking time: 20 minutes, plus cooling and drying

1 × quantity lemon cupcake mixture
(see Citrus Cupcakes, page 18)

For the icing and decoration

1 × quantity glacé icing (see Valentine
Cupcakes, page 152)

gel food colourings

2 tbsp royal icing (see page 162)

edible glitter (optional)

dragees (multicoloured if possible)

1 Make the cupcakes following the instructions on page 18. Leave to cool completely before decorating.

2 For the icing, make up the glacé icing and add deep navy blue food colouring to imitate the night sky. Leave the icing to dry completely. Separate the royal icing into as many bowls as you want colours, and tint them accordingly with the food colouring. Insert fine nozzles into several piping bags, fill with the icings and pipe on whatever firework you like, such as Catherine wheels, rockets and shooting stars.

3 Sprinkle a tiny bit of edible glitter over them, if you like, and add the dragees, which may need a tiny dab of royal icing underneath them to hold them in place.

Makes about 12

Christmas Cupcakes

Hands-on time: 20 minutes
Cooking time: 20 minutes, plus cooling and setting

50g (2oz) raisins

2 tbsp rum or brandy

125g (4oz) glacé cherries

125g (4oz) unsalted butter, softened

125g (4oz) golden caster sugar

2 large eggs

125g (4oz) self-raising flour

1 tsp baking powder

½ tsp mixed spice

For the icing and decoration

1 × quantity fondant icing (see Star
    Cupcakes, page 120)

2 tbsp royal icing (see page 162)

silver dragees

1 Put the raisins and rum or brandy into
a small bowl and put to one side for
1 hour. Preheat the oven to 180°C
(160°C fan oven) mark 4. Line a 12-hole
muffin tin with paper muffin cases.
Rinse the glacé cherries, pat dry and
then roughly chop.

2 Put the butter and sugar in a bowl and
beat together until light and fluffy.

Using a hand-held electric whisk,
beat the eggs in a separate bowl and
gradually add to the butter and sugar
mixture, beating well between each
addition. Add the contents of the bowl
containing the soaked raisins and
beat well.

3 Sift the flour, baking powder and
mixed spice on to a large plate and toss
the chopped cherries into the flour.
Carefully add to the wet mixture and
fold in with a large metal spoon. Spoon
carefully into the paper cases and bake
for 20 minutes or until golden and firm
to the touch. Transfer to a wire rack and
leave to cool completely.

4 For the icing, make up the fondant
icing and use to ice the cupcakes.
Leave to set.

5 Insert a fine nozzle into a piping bag
and fill the bag with royal icing. Pipe
Christmas tree shapes on to the cakes.
Add silver dragees to the trees as
decoration.

Calorie Gallery

160 cal ♥ 1g protein
6g fat (4g sat) ♥ 0.3g fibre
26g carb ♥ 0.2g salt
14

250 cal ♥ 4g protein
15g fat (9g sat) ♥ 0.4g fibre
29g carb ♥ 0.3g salt
16

259 cal ♥ 3g protein
17g fat (10g sat) ♥ 0.4g fibre
24g carb ♥ 0.4g salt
18

405 cal ♥ 5g protein
21g fat (11g sat) ♥ 1g fibre
53g carb ♥ 0.4g salt
20

203 cal ♥ 2g protein
14g fat (8g sat) ♥ 0.7g fibre
19g carb ♥ 0.2g salt
34

170 cal ♥ 2g protein
7g fat (4g sat) ♥ 0.5g fibre
26g carb ♥ 0.2g salt
36

332 cal ♥ 4g protein
21g fat (9g sat) ♥ 1g fibre
32g carb ♥ 0.4g salt
38

309 cal ♥ 4g protein
1g fat (trace sat) ♥ 0.8g fibre
76g carb ♥ 0g salt
52

408 cal ♥ 4g protein
24g fat (14g sat) ♥ 0.6g fibre
49g carb ♥ 0.5g salt
54

323 cal ♥ 3g protein
14g fat (8g sat) ♥ 0.8g fibre
50g carb ♥ 0.4g salt
56

452 cal ♥ 4g protein
31g fat (19g sat) ♥ 0.6g fibre
40g carb ♥ 0.7g salt
70

306 cal ♥ 3g protein
14g fat (8g sat) ♥ 0.6g fibre
46g carb ♥ 0.4g salt
74

282 cal ♥ 3g protein
13g fat (8g sat) ♥ 0.5g fibre
41g carb ♥ 0.3g salt
76

506 cal ♥ 3g protein
27g fat (17g sat) ♥ 1g fibre
66g carb ♥ 0.2g salt
78

409 cal ♥ 5g protein
g fat (11g sat) ♥ 1g fibre
43g carb ♥ 0.5g salt

385 cal ♥ 4g protein
26g fat (16g sat) ♥ 1g fibre
36g carb ♥ 0.2g salt

24

388 cal ♥ 4g protein
29g fat (18g sat) ♥ 1g fibre
30g carb ♥ 0.4g salt

26

306 cal ♥ 5g protein
18g fat (7g sat) ♥ 1g fibre
30g carb ♥ 0.4g salt

30

327 cal ♥ 4g protein
g fat (8g sat) ♥ 2g fibre
48g carb ♥ 0.3g salt

336 cal ♥ 5g protein
10g fat (2g sat) ♥ 2g fibre
57g carb ♥ 1.5g salt

44

338 cal ♥ 6g protein
23g fat (10g sat) ♥ 1g fibre
31g carb ♥ 0.4g salt

48

410 cal ♥ 4g protein
23g fat (14g sat) ♥ 1g fibre
51g carb ♥ 0.7g salt

50

404 cal ♥ 4g protein
fat (10g sat) ♥ 0.8g fibre
63g carb ♥ 0.4g salt

215 cal ♥ 3g protein
10g fat (6g sat) ♥ 2g fibre
31g carb ♥ 0.2g salt

60

480 cal ♥ 4g protein
25g fat (15g sat) ♥ 1g fibre
65g carb ♥ 0.6g salt

62

386 cal ♥ 4g protein
17g fat (11g sat) ♥ 0.8g fibre
58g carb ♥ 0.5g salt

64

316 cal ♥ 3g protein
g fat (8g sat) ♥ 0.6g fibre
50g carb ♥ 0.3g salt

246 cal ♥ 2g protein
10g fat (2g sat) ♥ 0.5g fibre
40g carb ♥ 0.4g salt

82

542 cal ♥ 9g protein
33g fat (13g sat) ♥ 2g fibre
56g carb ♥ 0.6g salt

84

294 cal ♥ 5g protein
13g fat (6g sat) ♥ 2g fibre
42g carb ♥ 0.1g salt

86

317 cal ♥ 5g protein
20g fat (10g sat) ♥ 2g fibre
34g carb ♥ 0.2g salt
92

360 cal ♥ 4g protein
16g fat (10g sat) ♥ 1g fibre
54g carb ♥ 0.5g salt
96

226 cal ♥ 3g protein
10g fat (6g sat) ♥ 0.8g fibre
34g carb ♥ 0.2g salt
98

361 cal ♥ 3g protein
14g fat (6g sat) ♥ 1g fibre
58g carb ♥ 0.2g salt
100

367 cal ♥ 3g protein
15g fat (8g sat) ♥ 0.7g fibre
55g carb ♥ 0.4g salt
114

287 cal ♥ 2g protein
6g fat (4g sat) ♥ 1g fibre
61g carb ♥ 0.1g salt
116

276 cal ♥ 4g protein
10g fat (4g sat) ♥ 1g fibre
46g carb ♥ 0.4g salt
118

226 cal ♥ 2g protein
10g fat (6g sat) ♥ 0.4g fibre
34g carb ♥ 0.4g salt
120

317 cal ♥ 4g protein
13g fat (2g sat) ♥ 0.6g fibre
49g carb ♥ 0.1g salt
132

363 cal ♥ 8g protein
17g fat (7g sat) ♥ 1g fibre
49g carb ♥ 0.5g salt
134

357 cal ♥ 4g protein
21g fat (13g sat) ♥ 0.6g fibre
41g carb ♥ 0.5g salt
136

171 cal ♥ 2g protein
7g fat (4g sat) ♥ 1g fibre
28g carb ♥ 0.1g salt
138

289 cal ♥ 2g protein
15g fat (9g sat) ♥ 0.4g fibre
40g carb ♥ 0.3g salt
150

291 cal ♥ 3g protein
12g fat (3g sat) ♥ 0.5g fibre
46g carb ♥ 0.5g salt
152

107 cal ♥ 1g protein
5g fat (3g sat) ♥ 0.3g fibre
16g carb ♥ 0.1g salt
154

563 cal ♥ 8g protein
34g fat (11g sat) ♥ 1g fibre
60g carb ♥ 0.3g salt
156

374 cal ♥ 4g protein
g fat (13g sat) ♥ 0.7g fibre
43g carb ♥ 0.6g salt
6

309 cal ♥ 3g protein
14g fat (8g sat) ♥ 0.6g fibre
46g carb ♥ 0.4g salt
108

374 cal ♥ 5g protein
18g fat (11g sat) ♥ 2g fibre
52g carb ♥ 0.4g salt
110

256 cal ♥ 4g protein
8g fat (1g sat) ♥ 1g fibre
45g carb ♥ 0.2g salt
112

375 cal ♥ 2g protein
g fat (12g sat) ♥ 0.4g fibre
50g carb ♥ 0.6g salt

424 cal ♥ 3g protein
19g fat (12g sat) ♥ 0.6g fibre
64g carb ♥ 0.6g salt
126

360 cal ♥ 5g protein
20g fat (11g sat) ♥ 1g fibre
45g carb ♥ 0.5g salt
128

283 cal ♥ 4g protein
12g fat (4g sat) ♥ 1g fibre
42g carb ♥ 0.2g salt
130

39 cal ♥ 0.4g protein
g fat (1g sat) ♥ 0.1g fibre
7g carb ♥ 0g salt

398 cal ♥ 4g protein
20g fat (13g sat) ♥ 0.9g fibre
53g carb ♥ 0.5g salt
142

233 cal ♥ 2g protein
10g fat (2g sat) ♥ 0.4g fibre
36g carb ♥ 0.4g salt
144

223 cal ♥ 2g protein
10g fat (6g sat) ♥ 0.4g fibre
34g carb ♥ 0.2g salt
146

515 cal ♥ 4g protein
g fat (18g sat) ♥ 1g fibre
57g carb ♥ 0.7g salt

254 cal ♥ 2g protein
10g fat (2g sat) ♥ 0.4g fibre
42g carb ♥ 0.4g salt
166

268 cal ♥ 2g protein
10g fat (6g sat) ♥ 0.7g fibre
45g carb ♥ 0.4g salt
168

Index

PICTURE CREDITS

Photographers: Steve Baxter
(pages 107 and 155); Nicki Dowey
(pages 35, 37, 57, 75, 137, 141 and
147); Brian Hatton (page 113);
William Lingwood (pages 19, 39,
69, 73, 83, 109, 121, 123, 139, 145,
153, 167 and 169); Myles New (page
51); Martha Pavlidou (pages 71 and
159); Craig Robertson (pages 12,
13, 17, 29, 33, 46, 47, 89, 90 and 91);
Lucinda Symons (pages 15, 21, 23,
25, 31, 43, 45, 47, 53, 55, 59, 61, 63,
65, 77, 81, 85, 87, 93, 97, 99, 101, 111,
115, 117, 119, 127, 129, 131, 133, 135,
143, 151, 157, 163, 164 and 165); Kate
Whitaker (pages 27 and 79).

Home Economists:
Joanna Farrow, Emma Jane Frost,
Teresa Goldfinch, Alice Hart, Lucy
McKelvie, Kim Morphew, Aya
Nishimura, Bridget Sargeson and
Mari Mererid Williams.

Stylists:
Tamzin Ferdinando, Wei Tang,
Helen Trent and Fanny Ward.

BAKE ME A CAKE
There's always time for cake

EASY PEASY MEALS
Easy meals for every day

LET'S DO BRUNCH
Mouth-watering meals to start your day

CHEAP EATS
Budget-busting ideas that won't break the bank

WONDERFUL ONE-POTS
Easy peasy recipes made in just one pot

Available online at store.anovabooks.com and from all good bookshops

SUPER SOUPS
Sumptuous soups for every day

SKINNY SUPPERS
Delicious, nutritious recipes under 300 calories

SLOW STOPPERS
Slow-cooked meals packed with flavour

GREAT VEG
Inspired ideas for delicious veggie meals

AL FRESCO EATS
Easy grills, barbecues and picnics

ROAST IT
There's nothing better than a delicious roast

FLASH IN THE PAN
Spice up your noodles and stir-fries

GLUTEN-FREE AND EASY
Oh-so-good-for-you recipes that taste great

LOW FAT LOW CAL
Nice recipes don't need to be naughty